Beginner to Overlander

Andrew Pain

Published by 721 Publishing
Copyright 2017, All rights reserved
IBSN - 978-0-9973480-9-5

Introduction

It was fall, 2015 I think, and I was at a Horizons Unlimited event in North Carolina. It was a nice night. Well there might have been some drizzle but a hurricane had passed by the week before so a slight drizzle wasn't anything to notice. I was hanging out by the fire with a cup of wine, friends, and a woman I was going to be marrying soon. The event organizer brought over someone to meet me. This person, whose name I am ashamed to have forgotten, wanted to start long distance, overland motorcycle traveling. He had some questions, and Mike (the organizer) thought I was the guy to ask.

Thinking this was going to be a quick conversation, I ducked out from the fire and we all started talking. It wasn't a quick conversation. The three of us moved around the venue, looking at motorcycles, going in and out of drizzle when it worsened to rain. Questions were asked and I answered them all as best I could. At the end, Mike apologized for pulling me away, but he'd thought I was the best person to help this new rider, and I was honored he'd thought so. I'd been making it a point to learn everything I could about Overlanding, doing what I could to encourage people to start traveling, showing it was nowhere near as difficult, dangerous, or expensive as so many people thought.

As we split up, Mike mentioned, perhaps next year, I could do a class on how to start overlanding - all the stuff someone wants to know before that *first* trip - all those things we wished we had known before our first trip. Since I liked the topic and didn't think it through (because overthinking is a terrible trait in an Overlander), I said sure and went back to find my future wife already in bed and more than a little upset at my disappearance. Obviously, we have made up. But that night in the drizzle was the start of this book.

I do remember my first trip. It was in the early 90s, before cell phones or the modern internet. I had a 1980 Yamaha SR250, blue, which I'd already crashed once and rebuilt the front with a SR500 (which had a larger front wheel and disk brakes). I didn't know much about motorcycles, and while I'd read some books from the library, it was still a topic there just wasn't much available about (beyond stories from the road). I had read *Zen and the Art of Motorcycle Maintenance* in High School, and since then I'd wanted to travel on a motorcycle. Now it was after college, and my mother (who thought motorcycles were death machines) could no longer stop me. I had been living with them, so I got the quiet recrimination and disapproval parents are good at, when their children have grown past the point they can be bullied or browbeat.

The morning I started was cold and damp. I left before anyone was awake, or at least up and moving. I thought that would make it easier, and I suppose it did. I wasn't out of the city before the rain started.

I didn't have good riding gear. I had a helmet, a school letter jacket (which wasn't waterproof, at least not waterproof enough). Khaki pants and hiking boots. My luggage was simply two backpacks I'd sown together, with my sleeping back in a trash bag behind me. The rain soaked me to the skin, and I got cold. Very cold.

I stopped in a rest area off the freeway, outside of the city. I had only been on the road for a bit more than an hour. The sun was, technically, up, but everything was gray and damp. I didn't have a stove, so sat in front of the heater vent in the building, trying to drink a cold coke, wondering what I was doing. I mean, what *was* I *DOING?* I could go home. Maybe leave again in a few days when the weather was better, or after I had better gear. There would be hot food, warm drinks. That I'd come back, and so quickly, wouldn't be mentioned, and I could prep better and leave again.

But I wouldn't leave again. Not on a motorcycle. Not on a trip like this one, open ended to where I wanted to go and see or end up. I knew that too.

So, I went back out, and got back on the motorcycle, and kept going. Through the rain and cold, heading away from home.

By lunch the sun had come out. I was further south and west by then, and it warmed up so much, when I stopped to camp that night, everything was dry. I found a pay phone and called to say I was still alive, and about where I was. I didn't mention the rain or doubt, but I didn't forget.

Every overland motorcyclist I've had this conversation with, has had *this* moment - usually early in their travels. That time when their experience, their equipment, their knowledge and confidence wasn't up to the challenge at hand. When the whole idea of overland travel seems terrible, and home and bed is calling.

8

Austin Grossman wrote a book called *Soon I will be Invincible*. The book has a line which goes something like "when you are faced with something you can *not* get through, but you get through it anyway, the person you are afterwards isn't the same. It's the person who *could* get through it." Of course, he was talking about someone turning into a super villain, but the basic idea is sound. It's why experienced Overlanders are such a competent bunch. Over and over, we are faced with things we can't do, but we have to do them anyway. Getting through borders, finding food and lodging, dealing with breakdowns and injuries, things which we learned to deal with because there wasn't a choice, until we became the people who could do them.

I don't know if this book will be able to elevate you to that level of confidence. Perhaps not. But I hope it will show you it *can* be done, and that you can do it.

In the end, all the books in the world won't make up for actually getting out there and traveling. So, no matter how great this book is it can't make you into an Overlander. I hope this book will give you a start, get you moving in the right direction, and give you confidence to overcome that first challenge - sitting in a rest area in the rain, wondering if you should just turn back. The road, the whole world, isn't behind you - it's forward. Just Go.

It isn't the mountains ahead to climb that wear you out. It's the pebble in your shoe. - Muhammad Ali

Training

You are your greatest asset. Put your time, effort and money into training, grooming, and encouraging your greatest asset. - Tom Hopkins

Language

If you talk to a man in a language he understands, that goes to his head. If you talk to him in his language, that goes to his heart. - Nelson Mandela

What's needed

I admit it - the first time I rode into Mexico, I only knew how to ask where the bathroom was. No, I didn't know how to ask for a beer. Since I crossed into Baja, this wasn't much of a problem early on. Northern Baja, even off the main highways, is close enough to the USA someone always spoke a little English. By the time I'd gotten far enough south where I had to work out what to say on my own, I'd figured out how to make myself understood, though that wasn't the same as being able to communicate.

How important is it to learn the local language? That's harder to answer than you would think. I spent months in Spanish speaking countries with little or no Spanish (I often say my Spanish is just about right for getting through a border or finding somewhere to sleep, but not much else), so clearly you don't *need* to know the local language - however there are times it can be lonely or frustrating not to be able to communicate freely with others. The loneliness you can address by finding other overlanders and talking to them (assuming you share a language with them, of course), but I remember needing to find a mechanic to fix a leaking fuel petcock on my motorcycle. I thought I knew the word I wanted, but I had no idea how to say it, and writing it down didn't help. Pointing and gesturing only got me polite looks.

In the end, I had to let it leak for a few more towns until I lucked into finding a motorcycle shop.

There is, now, another alternative. Apps for smart phones can work as translators, allowing some communication where otherwise there would be none. Pay attention to the app you invest in, to make sure it offers translation offline (so you don't need data services on your phone for it to work - otherwise in remote areas it won't work). I've never used one, so I don't have any direct experience, yet I've heard from others everything from how much they hate it to how invaluable it is - so your experiences may vary.

If you don't want to use an app, and want to learn the language so you have some idea of what is going on, how much do you really need? First, try to find an actual class, rather than a book or recorded audio. Learning how to say a stock set of phrases is of limited use, since eventually someone is going to answer you, and unless they manage to say something you recognize you will be in the same position as not knowing the phrases you learned. With some practice at conversation with different speakers you will have a better chance to understand when locals reply to you, or how to say and understand other words you encounter on your travels.

There is no easy way to know what words you will need to have once you are on the road, but directs (north, south, left, right, etc) are good to know, as well as some border words, such as customs. And where the bathroom is.

Immersion schools

In many countries - especially those with a strong tourist industry - there are options for immersion schools. While they vary in details, the idea is that you live with locals and work on learning the language every day - like going to school. Most know that you are there to see the area and it's not hours and hours every day, but it is a very good way to learn the language. You are encouraged, even forced, to speak and listen in the language all the times.

Many of the schools advertise online, and there are resources such as Lonely Planet that can help you find good ones. They vary from a family allowing you to live with them, and providing you with food and lodging while helping you learn, to more of a hostel setting, with other students and regular classroom learning, followed by going out and practicing in the town or city where the school is located.

As with most learning, you get out of it what you put in. A couple I knew taking a class in Guatemala stopped speaking in English with each other while in the class - which caused them some issues - but it meant they had to work on learning. There wasn't a time they could just 'turn off' and not keep trying. While this does help learn quickly (since there isn't any choice), it can also be frustrating and requires a lot of dedication on the part of the student to get the most out of it. Also, when staying with a family (as opposed to a more formal school-like arrangement), they may not know enough English to allow you to slack off at your learning. This may ultimately reward you with an excellent grasp of the language, but there will be a steep learning curve in the beginning.

Most schools include room and board with their fee, so you have somewhere to stay and meals, allowing you to focus on learning and exploring the town or city. The fees are more than you might spend normally for food and lodging, but you do also get the language lessons - and knowing the language might actually help you save money in markets or other areas.

On the other side of the speaking coin, so to speak, is teaching English while you are traveling. It doesn't always pay very much, but native English speakers are in demand all over the world, either for short classes lasting a month or two, to a year spent working with a local school or training center. This not only allows you stay somewhere, usually free, but you can earn money and have a chance to interact with the locals on a much deeper level.

Most places that hire English teachers require some sort of certification, which does take a little bit of time and money to earn, but once you have it, this means of travel opens up to you. The certification is available online, with classes to take and a fee. Once you have that, other sites will help you find work anywhere in the world you are looking to travel.

Medical and Health

Take some time to learn first aid and CPR. It saves lives, and it works. - Bobby Sherman

The Basics

Whether you are traveling on your own or with a group - either a tour group or a group of friends - you should have an amount of basic medical training.

How much training is that? Well, the simple answer is "however much training you feel you need to be comfortable on the road." One thing this book is intended to do is get you comfortable getting on the road and traveling. Ultimately, how much medical training will make you comfortable is up to you, but I do (of course) have some suggestions. I can even sum it up with just four words.

CPR and First Aid.

I know some of you are looking at an adventure magazines and the ads for medical training, and it looks like you *really need it* before you leave. Before you spend the money, here are a few things to consider. When you are traveling, it's more likely that you will be sick, rather than injured. Also, that the illness will be minor - stomach ailments are so common there are fun nicknames for them, like Delhi Belly. For that, you won't need any sort of medical training, just make sure you have the right medications along with.

That isn't to say that you won't have injuries, or be at risk for them. But, again, most of those injuries are going be minor and simple bandaids will deal with them. If there are serious or life threatening injuries, first aid training will allow you to treat and stabilize the injured person until medical help can arrive - that is what the training is for. CPR as well, for times when you need more than bleeding control or a limb splinted.

I remember when I took Emergency Medical Technician training for first time. I had been surprised at how much my first aid and CPR training had already covered. The things that were 'new' - toxicology (poisons and bites) and delivering babies - are of limited use for overlanders. While the toxicology might seem important, most animal and insect toxins are specific to local regions and require anti-venoms if they are dangerous to humans. Lucky for us, not many of them are, but it's impractical to carry all the needed medications around. Bite kits are available, and don't even need first aid training to be effective.

So let's say something serious does happen - an accident with a broken leg. First aid will control any bleeding and splint the leg - and then what? There will have to be some sort of interface with local medical care. This is true of just about any serious injury - local medical care will be needed. Most of the world has some sort of medical services available, and in a lot of those areas it's pretty good. Where there are people, they get injuries, and those need to be cared for.

Most of the problem for overland motorcyclist who are seriously injured isn't the care they need, but getting them to that care. Take the leg fracture - he's not going to be able to ride a bike. Again, being willing to accept local help is very,

very important for any overland traveler. Someone will know where the medical care is, and how to get there.

While you can take things like wilderness medical training, and while that training does have some merit, you are going to need locals more than you going to need to know how to build a stretcher, and finding a vehicle to put the injured party in will be better than carrying or dragging.

So, to repeat, while I am never going to discourage addition training, especially if you feel you need it to get on the road in the first place, all you really *need* to have to start overlanding is first aid and CPR. While the American Heart Association offers a CPR course (they call it BLS), I suggest taking the Red Cross version. It's a little more user-friendly and you can usually find weekend long courses for both trainings. As always, if you are traveling with a group, sign up together. You might get a group discount, and it makes sure everyone has the training needed, rather than having one medically trained person who might be the one injured.

Advanced Training

So, I just went on and on about how you really only need first aid and CPR to travel, but I also said there were limits to that training. Since one of the goals of this whole book is getting you over whatever is stopping you from traveling, I need to touch base on other trainings you might consider before hitting the road.

Now, just to repeat, all you really need is CPR and first aid. Don't forget that, but if you want more then by all means go and get more. If you think you need to get a Medical Doctor degree before you start traveling, I am not going to say you don't, only that you might be starting out with a lot of debt.

So, on a more practical level, what other training should you be considering? Since most of the concerns I hear from people not getting on the road are injuries in remote areas, training in wilderness or remote care is the obvious choice. There are training services spread around North America which offer such training, either to professional rescuers or laypersons looking to expand their knowledge. Make sure you clarify what training, if any, is required before signing up for a class. If possible, also find out if they are following a standard curriculum (such as NOLS, the National Outdoor Leadership School, who specialize in wilderness training) or something they established "in house." There is nothing

21

inherently wrong with an in-house system, assuming it is well taught and covers the needed skills.

What are the needed skills? Well, they should include expansion of first aid to using non-standard materials ("improvising"), as well as transport of an injured person over terrain to medical care.

Now, I know you read that and thought, "Wow, that sounds important. I really think I need to know that before I start traveling." It would be useful, but remember - *It's mostly common sense and suggestions.* The things that are more technical will require special tools. While those tool might seem useful, if you start trying to carry everything which might be useful you won't have a lot of room left for things like - well - clothes. If you remain calm and think, you will be able to figure the things you need to do. Some of the classes, as well, are intended (for example) to aid injured parties within first world countries get from a remote area to where an ambulance or flight medical crew can arrive and take over care. If you are in central Africa somewhere, the rules will be slightly different, and that training less effective.

I want to be clear - if having advanced training would make you feel better about being on the road, then definitely, *absolutely,* get the training. The whole point is to get on the road and start the traveling. To travel you don't need advanced medical training, but if *you* need advanced medical training to start traveling, either for your piece of mind or to comfort loved ones, then get the training.

Mechanical Things

Our work is to keep cranking the flywheel that turns the gears that spin the belt in the engine of belief that keeps you and your desk in midair. - Annie Dillard

Basic Maintenance

It looks complicated - all those wires and hoses. And compact - perhaps there isn't anything showing at all but clean, precise engine and body panels. Well, my stuff is rarely clean, but there's no doubting the intimidating complexity of it all. Not to mention the anxiety of messing something up - which would lead to a lot more damage and repairs and expense than the cost of having someone else just deal with oil changes and other basic upkeep tasks.

So, probably better to just let them do it.

No.

Okay, I'll admit it - even now I get a little nervous when I open up a valve cover and start measuring things. It's something I *have* messed up from time to time, so the anxiety is well founded. But I still do it, on the regular schedule, even when I'm home and have a mechanic who would be more than happy to do it for me (for a fee).

So, why? It's not just cost savings (though that is considerable and adds up), but getting to *know* your motorcycle. Where things are, what needs to come off so you can get to something else. *How* those things come off. There is also a surprising amount of self-confidence to be gained by being able to take care of simple things on your own, especially when you are on the road.

Exactly what you need to learn to do will depend some on what you are riding. If you have the owner's manual than it should have a service schedule listing what should be changed, and when.

Think about your trip and about how many miles you will be traveling, then add about 50% to that distance and look at the various services you will have to do. Some of those things I don't try on my own, in particularly changing any bearings. But other things, brake pads and fluids, are usually simple enough to take care on your own. If you know a large service is coming up, you can find a service center or garage where you can put the motorcycle and work on getting everything done. If you need parts, having a shop can give you a convenient place to have them shipped. More on that later.

Don't wait until you are on the road to start, though. Start at home, preferable when you have a lot of time and another vehicle available. There might be tools or parts you will need that you don't have, and when that happens just add them to your tool kit.

Installing upgrades

I come from Montana, and in eastern Montana we have a lot of dirt between light bulbs. - Conrad Burns

What upgrades?

So, you got this great motorcycle and you want to totally trick it out for some serious overlanding. The massive brick of the Touratech catalog arrived in the mail, and you have that and Twisted Throttle's catalog open to the relevant pages for your make and model. You have paper for notes and you computer up and running to get some reviews and suggestions before ordering that first round of stuff. You're just waiting to hear what you need.

So what do you need? Nothing, probably.

Okay, no motorcycle is going to be completely perfect for spending months or years living on the road. I know that, I really do. But most motorcycles are going to have the things you *need* to travel on them for months or years, and that's important to understand when it's time to start buying things for the bike - the difference between *want* and *need*.

Most, almost all, of that stuff you want from those catalogs are *wants*. They're totally cool, not going to disagree, but the cost to buy them will quickly add up to months of travel time, and traveling is supposed to be the whole point. So, what are the things you do *need*?

Most of these things will be extras, not replacements. If your motorcycle has footpegs, you don't immediately need to buy new footpegs, no matter what your online forum of choice recommends (and it will recommend something be replaced immediately, if not the pegs then something else). Take some time with the motorcycle first, perhaps a couple thousand miles and a few long weekend trips, before you start replacing parts.

But what about *adding* parts? Most of the things you should be buying early on are to *add* something to the motorcycle it doesn't already have. So, what doesn't your motorcycle have? If you bought one of those "Adventure Motorcycles" you see on all the YouTube videos and cool posters, then odds are you don't have luggage (you could get luggage, depending on the package you buy, but be careful with that. Aftermarket options are usually less expensive and at least as good, if not better, depending on your model). Unless you are going *really* minimalist (in which case all you need is somewhere for your toothbrush), you are going to need to carry things. On a motorcycle, that's luggage. You will want at least two side bags and some sort of tail bag (which goes on the rear seat or rack), but I prefer a five bag system I'll cover later.

Another important item to install, if you don't already have one, is a dedicated voltmeter - especially if you are attaching a lot of other electronics (like GPSs, phones, cameras, etc) or plan to use heated gear while riding. Even if you aren't planning on using the motorcycle's free electricity to keep things charged while riding, having something which can tell you there might be a problem with your electrical/charging system could be the difference between getting it fixed in a nice town, or needing to find someone to pick you up after your battery dies.

You will probably also want somewhere to mount a GPS. I am not a fan of GPS for *navigation*, but I think they are helpful for seeing where you are, in relation to where you want to be going (or, since my motorcycle doesn't have a tripmeter, how far I've ridden since I last got fuel. I also don't have a fuel gauge. Yeah, hard core, I know). You may also want somewhere to mount action cameras (like a GoPro) on handle bars or rear frames, but again I want to point out you aren't *replacing* anything the motorcycle already has.

Now, as you're riding, some of those things on the motorcycle are going to break or wear out. Brake and clutch levers might snap and I seem to wear out footpegs (I don't get the spiky metal ones, since then I wear out my boot soles and would rather replace the pegs). Pretty much anything that sticks out is at risk when the motorcycle falls over. When this stuff breaks, then you get the new, fancier version (if you still want to by then). You would be buying a new one anyway, so the increased cost is slightly off-set.

I think the same rule should apply to shocks, tires, all the parts on the motorcycle most forums suggest you replace as soon as you get the motorcycle home. Don't rush on all that spending, travel some instead. See what works for you (and what doesn't) and focus on getting the motorcycle ready for *your* trip - and don't forget that going on a trip is supposed to be the goal (not having the most aftermarket bits).

Repair and Maintain

Elsewhere I wrote about the importance of having the service manual for your motorcycle with you on the road. While you won't know how to do some, if not all, of the stuff contained within (personally, I am not looking forward to the first time I have to split the bottom cases open to get to anything in there), having the manual along means that anyone who *does* have to do those things (including you) has it available as a reference. It's hard to say how important that can be while on the road.

As you modify your motorcycle into your perfect overland travel machine, you are going to be moving away from that stock service manual. While that seems like an argument in favor of factory options, I don't mean for it to be. While factory options are nice, they *can be* more expensive than similar changes using aftermarket supplies. And remember, saving money on stuff means more money for doing things, and we want to be doers of things.

As you modify your motorcycle, you'll have to keep track of those changes in your service manual. This is important for when a mechanic unfamiliar with your machine is working on it and you aren't there (many large shops don't allow owners to tinker with their motorcycles in their workspaces, dealers are just about universally against it). Most of the aftermarket modifications will come with their own manuals, and these will have to be added to your service manual. If possible, note in the manual when the stock information no longer applies, and where to look for the updates. Of course, you might also be able to change the information in the service manual, but be careful about making too many changes on the pages. If you are constantly changing things you might find your book has become completely indecipherable. If the change is permanent, then you should change the information in the manual. More temporary changes (like different suspension) should have the relevant manuals attached. If you aren't sure, it's better to include the new manual rather than write in changes. I know, the books are bulky and hard to manage while traveling, but they really are worth bringing along. Of course, you should have digital backups somewhere, just in case.

So you bought a $1,000 rear shock, either because the stock one failed or you just needed the new suspension for whatever reason (better ricing, more weight, whatever). Hopefully that expensive new shock is rebuildable, but let's pretend that you really mangled it up. You need another one. You might be able to find a stock shock at a dealer (if there are dealers with your model, or *something* that uses the same shock), or even in a local shop. But the odds of finding that expensive aftermarket part on a shelf somewhere drop the further you get from a developed city (which also is the most likely place for you to have a problem with your shock). Of course, even in developed countries, inventory control means few dealers or shops will carry an expensive aftermarket part, or even a stock one. They will probably have a much easier time getting the stock shock in, though, in a reasonable amount of time. Since your aftermarket shock uses the same mounts, you should be okay to put the stock back on until you need to change it again.

But you wanted to lower or raise the rear of your machine, so you changed your mounts or ordered a difference size. Now you have to explain, while you need a rear shock, you don't need the one in the book, or one in that size, but something different. Hopefully you have good command of the language, or have the right documentation along.

Obviously, if you make changes to something more complicated than the rear shock (which is about as simple as it comes), *and* those changes mean you can't use stock replacement parts, this might cause issues down the road. While you could carry spares, starting to buy and carry two of everything you've change and might need to replace will quickly get expensive - both in terms of financial cost and weight and space. This is another reason to try and keep as close to stock as possible. It will keep the repairs as straightforward as possible while giving you the best chance to find replacement parts as needed.

Repairs

There is one advantage to having nothing, it never needs repair. - Frank Howard Clark

Mechanical

Things will go wrong. No matter how careful we are while traveling, and most of us are pretty careful (since needlessly damaging our stuff leads to increased costs in both money and time), things break. There is a temptation, when planning and packing to leave on that long trip, to cram your luggage full of spare parts and tools, hoping to be ready for everything that might go wrong while on the road.

Hopefully, you managed to take a simple course about small engines before you started on the road. If so, you probably got a sense of how many things there are to break, and the idea of carrying all those parts should've been a little daunting. You should carry replacements for things known to fail on your model motorcycle (most models that have been around for a while will have owner's forums, and owners will have worked out the weaknesses of your particular year and model - don't be afraid to ask, but expect to get a lot of recommended "improvements," which you might not really *need*). I carry a regulator/rectifier when traveling on my SR250. They just fail, randomly, and as a solid state hunk of plastic and metal there isn't much I can do on the road to repair it. Lucky for me, it's an inexpensive part and small enough I don't notice that I have it (until I need it, anyway). Odds are your motorcycle will have a similar part (or parts) that are a known weakness, and with luck it will be something you can easily carry. If not, try to plan ahead and have replacements ordered and shipped to stops along your route. You can then change it out regularly to prevent (hopefully) an awkward failure.

On the subject of easy-to-carry replacements, I cover elsewhere carrying tube and tire changing items. It's also worth packing spare levers for your clutch and front brake, and gear shift lever. Again, these are small items (I usually zip-tie the levers to the frame somewhere out of the way, where they are unlikely to be damaged in a fall (pro tip - put them on the opposite side of the motorcycle, so the gear shift lever is attached to the frame on the right side. One fall won't damage both)), and having one handy can make a huge difference. And, if you really want to order that fancy carbon-fiber or brushed aluminum lever from the catalog of your choice (even though I said you shouldn't), you can install that one and pack the OEM as your spare. So, it's almost a double win.

If your motorcycle has cables (mine does, but it's less and less common), carry a set of replacements. I usually try to run my cables through my frame so, when one breaks (not common, but it does happen) it's only a couple minutes to swap out both ends. If you chose to try this as well, remember to keep the spare cables lubed up. They tend to need it more than the ones actually in use. Also, if you have a drum front brake, be very careful with that cable so it doesn't get caught up in the spokes (I don't have that spare pre-placed). If, instead, you have hoses, consider braided steel for a replacement when the time comes. They are more durable, and perform better - but don't replace your stock hoses until you need to.

If your motorcycle has a chain drive, you will also need to have the tools and parts to repair it. If your chain has a masterlink, you should have a spare, as well as a chain link tool. If you don't have a master link, replacing your chain on the road will require a shop (or at least some serious tools), but it might be worth carrying a masterlink of the correct size just in case you have damage but can't get a complete chain. Masterlink chains are commonly thought to be not as strong as riveted chains (and they do have a point), but they are strong enough for most overland applications (where you aren't trying to maximize the power to the rear wheel), and much easier to deal with on the road.

Of course, chains are only one of the possible drive options. A shaft drive bike will require maintenance to keep working (usually an oil change), though there are some models where the shaft itself has to be replaced on a regular basis. That can usually be scheduled, and easy to plan for (if expensive and somewhat complicated). The last are belt drives, which are newer and rare on bikes tagged as "adventure motorcycles." That doesn't mean that bikes don't have them, and since you don't need an "adventure motorcycle" to travel, you might have a model with a belt. I *strongly recommend* carrying a spare belt along if you are planning to travel internationally, even if you are staying in developed countries. There is no guarantee you will be able to get a replacement easily. Your model might not even be available (or come with a different drive) once you've crossed your first border.

If other things go wrong, there are small things you can bring along to "patch" or provide some temporary repair to get you and the bike somewhere for more permanent fixes. Duck tape is a common, classic example. The rolls are large, though, so only buy it when you need it, rather than traveling with it all the time. And, yes, I know about the trick of wrapping some tape around something so you don't have to carry the complete roll, but that assumes you are on a shorter trip (and that you still have a home), which is nice but not true for everyone. Liquid metal (like JB weld) and epoxy are options to fix holes in the crankcase (which needs to be in one piece to hold all that oil inside) or damaged bodywork, though it takes some time to set once applied. Despite this, it can work as well as traditional welding if done correctly, and can make the difference between the end of a trip and staying on the road.

Speaking about repairs - one of the reasons I don't carry duck tape is that I prefer to actually fix things rather than patch them. Patching is fine to get somewhere to complete a repair, and *repairs* are what's needed to stay on the road. Whenever I stop in a major city (I like museums, and cities are a good place to meet people and get a sense of where to head next), before leaving I fix everything I can on the motorcycle. Loose parts, burned out lights, small leaks - everything I can find wrong. I complete whatever servicing it needs at the same time. If I need a garage and mechanic I have a better chance of finding one in a city than a smaller town, though smaller towns are more likely to provide random local help. I fix as much as I can when leaving small towns as well, though it's harder to get things shipped in, or find parts that will work. Of course, if it's just tightening bolts and changing tires, that is simple enough to do anywhere. Don't put those little things off or you'll find they become much larger things.

Electrical

I'm going to be honest. I hate, absolutely *hate*, electrical problems. I frequently say, not entirely jokingly, that my loathing of electrical failures is why I like traveling on a 35 year old motorcycle with a dozen wires and a single fuse. If I didn't love electric start, I could probably cut the number of wires in half.

But, that doesn't mean electrical issues don't happen, and when they do we have to deal with them the same as anything else. I usually start with swearing, and then check the fuse.

Most modern motorcycles come with more than one fuse, and use the blade type, though they might be the smaller version than standard automotive fuses. While you probably have a fuse bank, there might be other fuses located in the wiring (Yamaha had a thing, for a while, of installing a master fuse near the battery, behind the solenoid, and not mentioning it in the owner's manual, though it was in the service manual). Try to learn where all your fuses are before leaving. While they are commonly available in most developed countries, it's a good idea to carry a couple along - at least the ones needed for keeping the engine running (main, and ignition, for example, rather than turn signals). Luckily they're small and cheap.

Speaking of small, cheap things to carry for electrical issues, learn how to remove those special connectors on your motorcycle's wiring harness. There is a trick to it, needing a small screwdriver, but once you know how it's simple. Your motorcycle will have a selection of these connectors, and carrying them all would be impractical. But you can buy and carry a couple, for connections needing two through four wires. The ends of the wires themselves are standard, so if you have problems with a connector you can replace both ends and (hopefully) get back on the road.

So how do you know what's wrong? Well, first you'll need the service manual, and then you'll need a voltmeter or multimeter. The multimeter is more generally useful, though it's more complicated (I don't know everything mine does, and use the internet for instructions on how to get it to check things that need checking - I *said* I wasn't good with electrical problems). As part of the small engine class you should have learned a few things about how to use a meter, but most of what you'll need while trouble shooting on the road will be specific to the model motorcycle you're riding. Some systems are also much more complicated than others, finding someone willing to go through everything before you leave (hopefully with you there to watch) can be very useful.

There are some motorcycles that come with onboard diagnostic systems. You just plug in your computer or a scanner (like the ones cars have had for years now), and it will give you a code (or something similar), which in turn will explain what's wrong. From there, you should be able to fix the problem (or order the parts to fix the problem) and get moving again. Obviously, if you have this option you should definitely be making use of it, though some scanners are expensive and others are simple plugs that attach to a computer (which means you are bringing along a computer with the relevant software installed).

Obviously, you can hope nothing goes wrong, and you might even be right, but it is better to put some thought into what you will do if something does go wrong. Modern motorcycles are considerably more complex than ones from even ten years ago (and, thankfully, more reliable), so learning how to diagnosis and repair electrical faults is extremely important.

Getting Help

It's not really a surprise to overlanders that, given enough time on the road, things are going to go wrong. And when I say things - I mean Things, with a capital T. Things you can't fix, Things you don't have the parts or tools or space or time for. Things that leave you on the side of the road, looking forlornly at your motorcycle and wondering what you were thinking when you cancelled your cable subscription, all that time (or that long) ago.

Don't panic. No, seriously, don't panic.

If you have food and water it's a good time to take a break. If you don't have food and water, you are in survival mode and need to get water as soon as you can (and you should, of course, never leave somewhere without having water, but that is for another section). Wait on the side of the road, look like you're stuck (parts off, tools out, etc). Someone will stop. No, really, someone will.

They might not be able to directly help, but perhaps they will know someone who can. Or maybe their phone works and they can call for help. If you just need fuel, maybe they will give you some. Once, while working on changing a flat in Ecuador, three men were walking past. They promptly took over the changing of my inner tube, and would only take one bottle of water (for the three of them) in exchange.

People are nice, (most of them, anyway).

42

Here is something to keep in mind. While we view ourselves and awesome adventures, self-contained in our own little traveling worlds, the truth is none of us, *none of us*, are really all that self-sufficient. No overlander can carry everything needed while traveling. It's important to be open and willing to accept help when it's offered (not just when it's needed) on the road. It's actually harder than you think, something I still struggle with (especially when everything is going well, and something like an offer of free lodging comes up).

This is especially true when things are going wrong, and you are getting frustrated or confused. The world is full of people and things, and (as I just mentioned), most of them are good and want to help if you let them. Use your common sense, and if something feels wrong or unsafe you have to trust your instincts, but don't let fear dictate what you do (especially if you are stranded somewhere). Let the locals help you get to a mechanic, find somewhere for you to stay, get you some food. They will know the area much better than you, and letting them direct you will get you to where you need to go much faster and easier than if you tried to figure it out on your own (probably).

Of course, there *are* bad people out there who will look to take advantage of you, so along with some common sense, do some other things as well. When you can, check in online or with a local overlander community (which also can be a great source of local help). They will either let you know you are on the right track or help you if you aren't. They might even be the locals who are already helping you, but if you are getting into trouble they are the ones who will know, and the ones most likely to come and help get you out of it.

If you need mechanical help, some shops will let you help with the repairs to your motorcycle, especially if it's a model they don't normally work on. This is where having the hard copy of the manual will come in handy, since both you and the locals can reference it. If they are letting you use their shop and tools, make sure to be respectful - especially with cleaning up after yourself, but also about eating or even how you dress. Pay attention to what they are doing and try to adapt and not offend. Even if you aren't perfect, trying will serve you better than ignoring their customs. I remember a story told by one overlander working in a garage in the middle east. He placed his helmet on the ground, which isn't uncommon. If it's on the ground it can't fall. This bothered the local Muslims, who find the ground unclean and didn't like his helmet there. While this may seem like a small thing, the rider moved his helmet to a table. It *was* a small thing, but it is their country, their garage, and moving the helmet was respectful and didn't cost the rider anything.

There will be other shops which don't let you, the rider, work on or even monitor what's going on. In this case, getting in touch with local riders is a *really* good idea, to find out whether the mechanics at that shop have any idea what they are doing. My local mechanic is in this group - if you need

44

him to work on your bike then he will work on it, but don't expect to hang out in the garage or be able to "help" - but he is also one of the best motorcycle mechanics, and his garage one of the best service locations, within a couple hundred miles. Handing over your transportation to someone can be scary, sometimes it's the only option. Try to do some research, but in the end, if you need help, you need help.

If there isn't help, or at least none that you can trust, then you are going to have work out something. Usually, this means you will have to figure out how to do the repair on your own. Try to get somewhere you can stay comfortably for a while and has a secure place to work. Good internet access is also a must, since you are going to spend a lot of time looking up what you are supposed to be doing. Vehicle specific forums are going to be your friend, unless you have a good mechanic back home you can call to help you work through what you need to do. Hopefully wherever you are stuck will have a decent hardware store, or places you can borrow tools from (again, don't be afraid to ask), and that you can get things shipped into if needed.

When I tried to ride through the Atacama desert without oil (not recommended, by the way), I found myself in this situation. The local mechanic thought I should sell my motorcycle (to him, I suspect, then buy a replacement from him as well), my mechanic back home talked me through a top-end rebuild over the course of several days (with delays while I got things I needed locally, and because I could only work a few hours a day. It gets very hot in the desert). The hostel staff helped me find the things I needed, and the whole staff came out to see if the bike started when I was done. It did, and I got dinner and the last night for free.

Leaving Work / Getting Time off

A vacation is what you take when you can no longer take what you've been taking. - Earl Wilson

About Taking Time

Before I start getting into leaving work for travel, I want to talk a little about time. Time and money are among the big reasons people usually give me when they say they can't travel *right now*, but they are going to start in the future. I am going to go over money later, but right now I want to talk about time.

I've heard, and had, conversations with people looking to take that long trip - longer than a vacation, long enough you need to do more than pack a few things in the morning - and I've heard it said over and over. "I don't have the time now, but I want to someday."

I was like that, at one point. I was working full time as a Paramedic, and taking more than a month off each yer to ride a motorcycle around. I had friends who were jealous of all that time off, though it came at a cost of long days and longer weeks when I was working. But I wanted to leave it all, to get away and start traveling full time. To see more of the world than I could even with four to six week chunks. I read the books, watched the shows, looked at the magazines, and dreamed about someday. Even after my father died from complications dealing with cancer, after my fiancee left me (well, I left her officially, but that is another story), after I spend years wondering what I was doing with my life.

Then, in 2009, I had a bad week at work. I was still working as a paramedic, but it wasn't anything gruesome or violent that caught my attention, focused my energy. It was a hospice transfer. The way the laws were at the time, hospice transports posed something of a problem for ambulance crews. We are, after all, trained, sworn, and legally obligated to try and save the life of anyone under our care. Hospice patients, though, are facing end of life illnesses and aren't looking to be saved, only kept comfortable. So there were only a few crews who got to do those transports, but there also weren't many of them (a couple a month), so it wasn't that big of a deal. Over a two week period (10 days, due to my schedule) I had three, but one was all that mattered.

He was older than me, but only a couple years. We picked up him and his wife from a hospital in the city to take them both home, where he was going to die. Most people want to die at home, so I guess he was getting his wish. He didn't talk, so I chatted with his wife during the ride. He had worked, worked a lot, and built a successful business. He'd cashed out the year before, and they were going to spend the rest of their lives together on the windfall. It was, in a nutshell, the dream so many people spend their lives chasing. Their driveway had a massive RV under a cover. It might have been larger than my apartment, and the house was definitely nicer. Full of those little knick-knacks that made us nervous rolling our cot around.

He didn't notice any of that. In fact, he was a shriveled husk, skin loose over bones. There was a IV pump dumping so much painkiller into his system it probably would have killed me. Six months earlier a regular checkup found cancer, and now there he was. The wife didn't know what to do, she didn't seem as excited about the idea of traveling, in fact she didn't seem excited about much of anything.

This guy, this couple, had done all the things they were supposed to have done to enjoy a long life on the road. They had worked to get the funds, they had sacrificed the earlier part of their lives on the promise they would have the later part, but they weren't going to. He wasn't, perhaps she would recover - I don't know. But I did know he wasn't much older than I was (younger than I am now), and that he wasn't going to get to travel. I wanted to travel, and realized then I couldn't keep putting it off, if I was really going to go.

We all have the time to travel. We all have time, none of us know how much time we have and won't until we run out, but *right now*, you have time. You are just *spending* that time on other things. And I mean spending - time, like money, is a resource we have to pay attention to. With money, though, we usually know how much we have, and some idea how to get more. Time doesn't work like that, and while we should treat it so much more preciously, we usually squander it as though it will never run out. I don't want to terrify you, but it will.

I know that it can be terrifying to leave home, family, friends, and work to set off on a long trip, without knowing how it will all end, and what you will do when it's over. I've tried, in this section, to give you some practical advise. But, really, taking this plunge isn't about any advice I can give you, it's about how you are choosing to spend the time you have.

Quit

Most people I know have had a time in their life when they wanted to quit their job. Those flashes of frustration aren't the same thing as seriously leaving work for months or years of travel. Most of us are used to having regular paychecks, as well as other benefits (health insurance is the big one for people from the Unites States). Quitting your job means giving all of that up, and it can be more than a little terrifying.

First, once you've decided you are going travel and are going to have to leave your job, you should start some sort of saving plan to cover your expenses while you are on the road. Start doing this even before you've fully worked out where you are going. Seriously, you can't start saving too early in this process. You might have a job which allows you to work remotely (and therefore while you are traveling), or a source of passive income, but I still recommend aggressive savings, starting as early as you can.

While savings will be important, some travelers will have passive income sources. If you aren't familiar with the term, passive income comes from sources that don't require you to check in to work on a regular basis (or do work at all). These can be investments, rental properties, retirement income, or money from a pyramid scheme you set up a few years ago. The point is that you don't have to invest much, if any, time in actually producing income.

Remote work is where you can get the work done from the road, or any other not-actually-at-work location. Freelance writing or design are common, though not always consistent, ways to earn while traveling, but depending on your current job, working remotely might be an option. Many employers like to see their employees on a regular basis, whether the work is being done or not. You will have to ask to see if remote work is a possibility.

And about asking. Everyone's work situation is different. I have been extremely fortunate with my employers allowing me to take off and wander around the planet from time to time, but I know not everyone is that lucky. Some employers might not even been excited about your plan to leave "in the future," and decide you should leave much sooner. Hopefully not, but I can't know everyone's work situation. If you are concerned about losing your job sooner than planned, then you are going to have to keep your employer in the dark about your plans to leave. Since (in other parts of this book) I will be encouraging you to tell everyone what you are planning, managing this might pose a problem. Again, you will have to decide for yourself the best way to deal with it, depending on what you know about your employer.

Hopefully, though, your employer is at best neutral and potentially positive about your plans to travel. If that is the case, or if you think it might be, then you should do everything you can to keep them in the loop for your plans. One of the wall maps I used to plan my route ended up in someone's office when I left, so they could follow my travels while I was on the road.

Maintaining that good relationship can also provide a benefit after your trip, which I'lll cover later. In general, if you have to leave your job to travel, then it's best not to burn any bridges before you go. You might not be planning on coming back, or going back to the same employer or even industry, but you never know what the road is going to bring, or where it will drop you at the end.

Time off

For some shorter trips, you might be able to take time off work, rather than simply quitting. Different employers will have different rules for this, either sabbaticals or leaves or just placing your work on hold, but if this is an option, you should seriously consider taking it.

While not quitting everything might seem like a cop out on your trip, don't think of it that way. There are some advantages to having a "home" while you are on the road. Some countries are less excited about issuing tourist visas to travelers if that traveler doesn't have somewhere to go back to (so they don't have to worry about you coming into the country on a easy-to-get tourist visa, then not leaving), and will ask at the border where you live and where you work. I was asked several times what I did for a living, and always answered that I was a paramedic in Wisconsin, No one asked for my employer information, but if they did I was ready to give it. Of course, I *had* left my job, so what might have happened if someone called is anyone's guess. Probably nothing pleasant.

Keeping your job also gives you a (perhaps small) safety net at the end of your trip. While it's been my, and others, experience that finding work after a long trip isn't nearly as hard as you might think, giving up the security of a job might be too big a jump for some travelers. Since I want everyone traveling, keeping your job while you are on the road is fine with me.

Before you get on too high a horse over someone keeping their job (or house, or whatever) while on the road for a long trip, remember that most travelers you meet while on the road will have jobs, and houses, and perhaps family, waiting for them when they get home. While there are a lot of overlanders who cut all their ties to the life they've been living before they start on the road, there are also a lot who don't - who are taking long trips for the trip's sake, not to restart their life.

There is also the middle ground of finding remote work while you are traveling, even though this isn't what you did before you started traveling, and might not be what you are planning to do when you get back. While it does mean investing time to find work and to actually do it once you've found it, there are websites that try to connect skilled freelancers with projects. How much you can earn at this depends on your skill set and the amount of time you are willing to put into it.

If you are keeping up a blog or vlog while traveling, you can also monetize that, keeping a "job" while on the road, as you will have to regularly produce content for the site. I do this, to a small extent, but I am not a fan of ads all over a website. In fact, I don't have any real ads, instead using links and reviews. It means I don't earn as much as I might be able to, but since I'd rather have a nice looking site and earn less than something covered in banners and flashing colors, I accept that.

If you are keeping your "real" job while traveling, odds are they will want to know when you plan to be back. If you are taking a leave of absence, a return date is usually required. I like open-ended travel, where you can go where you want, when you want, and stay as long as you want, but the simple truth is it's hard to maintain that sort of trip. If you plan to do any shipping, getting dates locked in as early as possible usually results in the best price, which also means you have those dates (where you need to be somewhere by a certain date) hanging over you. Needing to meet people for visiting, or to get out of a country before a visa expires, can also cause time pressure on a trip, so having to be home by a certain date isn't automatically worse than any of those. And, if your trip changes and you don't plan to go home, or can't make it home by the return date, you can address actually quitting (or rescheduling your return) then.

After The Trip

Before I start getting into leaving work for travel, I want to talk a little about time. Time and money are among the big reasons people usually give me when they say they can't travel *right now*, but they are going to start in the future. I am going to go over money later, but right now I want to talk about time.

I've heard, and had, conversations with people looking to take that long trip - longer than a vacation, long enough you need to do more than pack a few things in the morning - and I've heard it said over and over. "I don't have the time now, but I want to someday."

I was like that, at one point. I was working full time as a Paramedic, and taking more than a month off each yer to ride a motorcycle around. I had friends who were jealous of all that time off, though it came at a cost of long days and longer weeks when I was working. But I wanted to leave it all, to get away and start traveling full time. To see more of the world than I could even with four to six week chunks. I read the books, watched the shows, looked at the magazines, and dreamed about someday. Even after my father died from complications dealing with cancer, after my fiancee left me (well, I left her officially, but that is another story), after I spend years wondering what I was doing with my life.

Then, in 2009, I had a bad week at work. I was still working as a paramedic, but it wasn't anything gruesome or violent that caught my attention, focused my energy. It was a hospice transfer. The way the laws were at the time, hospice transports posed something of a problem for ambulance crews. We are, after all, trained, sworn, and legally obligated to try and save the life of anyone under our care. Hospice patients, though, are facing end of life illnesses and aren't looking to be saved, only kept comfortable. So there were only a few crews who got to do those transports, but there also weren't many of them (a couple a month), so it wasn't that big of a deal. Over a two week period (10 days, due to my schedule) I had three, but one was all that mattered.

He was older than me, but only a couple years. We picked up him and his wife from a hospital in the city to take them both home, where he was going to die. Most people want to die at home, so I guess he was getting his wish. He didn't talk, so I chatted with his wife during the ride. He had worked, worked a lot, and built a successful business. He'd cashed out the year before, and they were going to spend the rest of their lives together on the windfall. It was, in a nutshell, the dream so many people spend their lives chasing. Their driveway had a massive RV under a cover. It might have been larger than my apartment, and the house was definitely nicer. Full of those little knick-knacks that made us nervous rolling our cot around.

He didn't notice any of that. In fact, he was a shriveled husk, skin loose over bones. There was a IV pump dumping so much painkiller into his system it probably would have killed me. Six months earlier a regular checkup found cancer, and now there he was. The wife didn't know what to do, she didn't seem as excited about the idea of traveling, in fact she didn't seem excited about much of anything.

This guy, this couple, had done all the things they were supposed to have done to enjoy a long life on the road. They had worked to get the funds, they had sacrificed the earlier part of their lives on the promise they would have the later part, but they weren't going to. He wasn't, perhaps she would recover - I don't know. But I did know he wasn't much older than I was (younger than I am now), and that he wasn't going to get to travel. I wanted to travel, and realized then I couldn't keep putting it off, if I was really going to go.

We all have the time to travel. We all have time, none of us know how much time we have and won't until we run out, but *right now*, you have time. You are just *spending* that time on other things. And I mean spending - time, like money, is a resource we have to pay attention to. With money, though, we usually know how much we have, and some idea how to get more. Time doesn't work like that, and while we should treat it so much more preciously, we usually squander it as though it will never run out. I don't want to terrify you, but it will.

I know that it can be terrifying to leave home, family, friends, and work to set off on a long trip, without knowing how it will all end, and what you will do when it's over. I've tried, in this section, to give you some practical advise. But, really, taking this plunge isn't about any advice I can give you, it's about how you are choosing to spend the time you have.

Family

Learn to enjoy every minute of your life. Be happy now. Don't wait for something outside of yourself to make you happy in the future. Think how really precious is the time you have to spend, whether it's at work or with your family. Every minute should be enjoyed and savored. - Earl Nightingale

Coming With

So you want to travel with friends or family (or both). Sweet.

Traveling with others requires a larger commitment of time and energy than solo travel, whether you are planning months on the road with friends, or years on the road with a spouse or kids. No matter what else you might have heard or think, believe me - it's more work when you are not alone, if you want to make the relationships work, along with the trip.

If you are planning to travel with others, remember that you are traveling *with* them. So, during all the planning and prep, they need to be as involved. This includes making sure adult traveling companions are aware of each other's "must see" places, so there aren't surprises along the road, and to avoid disgruntled riders when the one thing they *really* wanted to see more than anything else gets skipped or missed. This is especially true if it happens after extra time was spent elsewhere, and even worse when the riders involved are children (chronologically, not emotionally), since they might not have understood more time at place A meant missing place B. There will be things that come up during route planning, and not everyone will get to see and do all the things they want. Be honest with each other about what is wanted from the trip - if traveling together isn't going to work, it's better to find out before leaving than after you are all on the road.

With children, the amount of involvement will depend a lot on their ages. While getting kids traveling while they are young is better, very young children obviously won't be able to help as much with planning. As they get older, especially if they have grown up with travel, they will be able to help with decisions about where to go, how long to spend there, and what they want to see or learn while on the road. As much as possible, these things should be worked into the travel plan, since keeping the kids involved and interested will pay off later.

If you are traveling with a significant other - spouse, boyfriend or girlfriend - be aware that traveling together is a whole different sort of relationship from being at home. For one thing, there will be a large reduction in personal space, and you will have a massive increase in the amount of time you spend together. While that might not sound all that bad, the truth is many relationships (even very strong ones) struggle under these conditions. Since relationships are different (and even with the number I've had, I'm no expert) I don't have a lot of advice other than to be honest with each other - even when that honesty is limited to being pissed off and wanting to be alone for a bit. And, if that is what your partner wants (which, usually, is just a request for some space), then allow it. There will be time to talk things out later, hopefully.

There are going to disagreements. If the trip evolves into something which one of person wants, but not the other, agree to split up for a while rather than forcing someone into something they aren't happy with. While being apart for a while might suck, it won't suck as badly as the recrimination or disappointment which will come if your partner (or you) end up not enjoying the trip, don't get to see or do the things you (or they) want to do. While you are trying to travel together, it's okay to be apart from time to time so you each get what you want from the trip - which is supposed to be the whole point, after all.

Of course, you might be lucky enough to have a partner who always agrees with you on what you want to see or do, and it's just a matter of planning it all out (or that your trip has enough time that there isn't any reason to compromise). Still make sure you work on what to see together, so your interests are both expressed as part of the route plan, and you both have input on where you are going and what you are going to see while you are there. This is also true (though perhaps a little less so) with children. Having them involved in route planning is a good way to make sure they stay interested in the trip during the planning stages (in my experience, it's no guarantee they stay interested while on the road, but it's worth a try), but make sure they don't encourage you to bite off more than you should as part of the trip. Remember to take *time* at the places you stop so you have the chance to really enjoy and experience them. If you are constantly having to move to a new location to see something else, you will end up not seeing nearly as much as you wanted to.

If you are traveling with kids and planning to be on the road for a *long* time, you're going to have to think about their education. Well, I guess you don't *have* to, but it might be worthwhile. Home schooling (at least in the United States) is becoming increasingly popular, and there are international equivalents. If you do live in the USA, check with your home state about their requirements. Most have basic subjects they want to you cover, and some sort of basic competency testing to make sure it's getting done. They might also have money (yay money!) which you can use to cover some of the expenses from education, since your child isn't getting their money back from public schools. What's actually needed, and what you have to provide, varies wildly from state to state, so if you are truly pulling up roots and don't know where you new "home" state will be, you can look at the requirements from different states before choosing a curriculum (though that will also set your "home" state while you are on the road - so you will need an address to convince that state you "live" there. Check with your extended family and see what your options are).

World Schooling is a slightly different beast. It's way more flexible and open, to the point of not using a curriculum at all, only suggested subjects of study. Probably because of this, it can cause some issues when returning to a "traditional" learning environment. Again, there are a lot of programs set up in World Schooling which you can follow, and you (as the parent and teacher) should keep records of the things taught and learned for later reference.

There was a time home schooled and world schooled students were at a disadvantage when looking at college, but that is less and less of an issue as more and more home school students "graduate" high school. While it might be easier to get into some colleges, compared to others, that is going to be the case no matter how your child learns. You can't just ignore it, but you can do some research and plan ahead.

Most home school programs will take little time every day to complete, allowing for more time to explore and experience things while traveling. Having said that, it will take some discipline on the part of the child and the parent to get the school work done. The maturity of the child might be a large factor in this, as well as what they are used to. Establish a routine early and stick with it - just like traditional schooling does - as much as your travel permits.

Leaving Them Behind

Sometimes, your loved ones just can't come with. It sucks, I am not going to lie about it, but (as I've told my wife), I can't stop traveling. While I miss her and always want her to come with, not getting on the road from time to time and exploring would kill me, or at least destroy some of the things she loves about me.

Of course, my wife also loves to travel, so the biggest hurdle for me is dealing with the fact she wants to come with but can't (usually because of family commitments). In that way I am lucky I guess.

If you have a spouse who doesn't want to travel, but is willing to let you go, do your best to include them in the parts of the journey you can. Send lots of pictures, post cards, ship and bring back gifts - you get the idea. Let her help with deciding where you are going to stay and what you are going to see, and (as much as you can) include her in these places while you are traveling. With some luck, over time, she will want to come along, dealing with the bad parts of travel in order to more fully enjoy the good times. My mother, who was quite sure I would be killed within months of starting to ride motorcycles, has actually followed my travels in this way - seeing through my eyes places she'd always wanted to see but never gotten to on her own.

I need to say this - I am using "her" and "she" a lot, but I know full well that it's not always the male who is traveling and the woman who stays behind. It's just awkward to try and use both pronouns. Since I'm male and a lot of what I'm writing is from my experience and research - well you get the idea.

So, moving on.

If your spouse is against the idea of travel, well you are in for a rough road. If you are intent on going anyway, you will have to decide for yourself whether or not you can involve her in the planning of the trip. I would think it's always better to include rather than exclude - but I will admit to not having experience dealing with a spouse that is obstructing travel. Perhaps you can win her into at least accepting, rather than opposing, with stories from other travelers or pictures of far-flung places.

You might, however, have a spouse who would love to come with, but can't. Mine, for example, has two girls in school. While we can take off and hit the road for the whole summer, we know we wouldn't be as good as we want to be about home schooling, and we aren't sure they would do well with the complete lack of structure. Other people hoping to travel might have elderly parents or someone else close to you with health issues, who you can't or don't want to leave. Even if this is the case, it doesn't mean you *can't* travel, only that you have to take care on how you plan and execute that travel. If you might need to return home suddenly, then you need to make sure your route takes you, regularly, to places where you can catch a flight if needed. You will also have to make sure you have connectivity with people back home, so you know when you need to come back.

If you aren't comfortable being away for a long time, focus on shorter trips. If you travel slowly, and really try to soak in wherever you are, rather than trying to reach somewhere and forcing yourself to keep moving, even a long weekend away can settle down your travel urges.

All The Stuff You've Already Bought

I've been a minimalist my whole life, even if you wouldn't know it from my office. - Neil deGrasse Tyson

No One Left Behind

You have stuff. Perhaps you have a lot of stuff. Perhaps some of it is really nice, probably most of it is just stuff which builds up around a life lived "normally." Toasters and microwaves, TVs and DVDs and kitchen chairs.

Very little of this stuff will come with when you start traveling. You are going to have to do something - probably sell some, give other things away, but there are going to be some things - heirlooms or family photos or something - which you can't get rid of. You are going to have to do something with them.

If you have someone who can store them for you (like a spouse who isn't coming with, for example, or a sibling who you trust to look after them), things are a little easier, but if there won't be anyone left behind when you leave home that last time, you will have to work out something else.

The best choice for things you want to keep, but not take along, is to have someone look after them, preferably a family member or very close friend. If you don't have anyone willing, or able, or that you trust, to take your things, you are going to have to arrange storage. Storage payments can eat into your travel budget, but it is a good way to keep things safe and secure while you are on the road. Many long term travelers have a storage locker somewhere with personal items (or other motorcycles) for when they are home.

If you live in a city where there are several storage options, make sure you shop around. Many offer deals for new customers, but the actual price per month can vary considerably. This is also true of units within the storage facility itself - I learned I could have 10 more feet of depth if my unit didn't have a loft (which was difficult to access) *and* pay $25 less a month (this was when I was "home" and needed somewhere to put a car when I wasn't using it). Don't be afraid to ask about rates on other units, as well as what hours you are allowed to access your unit (some close in the evenings) and if someone is on-site all the time. Some also offer insurance for the things being stored, though I don't know how much good that insurance would actually be. I haven't heard of anyone needing to cash in.

One other thing to consider when looking at storage units is how weather sealed it is. While many are just unheated garages, you can get some (usually inside a building) which are more protected from the elements. If you are storing fragile things, like photographs, this might be worth considering. These units are usually smaller and more expensive, so you will have to consider which will best suit your needs.

You should be careful not to get *too much* storage. Look at what's available and what you are looking to keep, and try to get the smallest you can. Don't go up a size, "just in case." While you might find things to fill the space, you will have to pay for that space while you are on the road. That extra $10 or $25 (or more) a month will add up over time, and it won't be easy to go home and move to a smaller unit if you decide you want that money for something else in your monthly budget. On the day you are "moving in" to your storage (this will probably happen over a few days, actually, close to your departure date), if you learn you can't fit everything into that 5x10 space, *then* ask about an upgrade.

You should also get a combination lock for your storage locker, not one that works with a key. Even if you don't have anyone behind to look after your stuff, odds are you know *someone* in town, and if something happens that requires access to the storage unit you can share your combination. This is a much easier than trying to handle key access. Take a picture of the combination and store it online with your other important documents, so in a year or two or ten you can look up the numbers yourself and get your stuff back.

Someone Left Behind

If you are going to leave whatever belongings you aren't selling, or gifting, with someone, congrats on having someone that stable in your life. Also, for saving a lot of money on storage you can spend on gas and food.

You should make sure that who ever is looking after your things is aware of what they are getting themselves into. Perhaps it's a spouse who can't or won't travel with you, or grown up kids who have space they can let you use. Whoever it is, you should talk with them about what you are looking to store with them, and what you are planning they to do with it. It should also be clear what is being *given* to them for use, and what you are asking them only to *store,* without their using it. Also, if they are the sort to move often or are renting, make sure whatever you are leaving with them won't be too much of a hassle to transport, or you'll find it didn't make the trip. Obviously, that would suck.

Get all your belongings boxed up and sealed, preferably in heavy duty plastic containers. These are easier to transport and store than cardboard boxes, and will last longer. Put a list of what's inside, if you can, on the lid. This way, if you need something from one of the boxes, it's easier for someone to find it. Don't over pack the boxes, so they can be lifted and moved easily.

If you are storing things like furniture or TVs, consider whether you want to make them available for use. Yes, they might be damaged and will probably be more worn than if simply stored, but larger things like this are hard to stick in an attic and not touch for a couple of years while you are on the road, so consider offering them. Odds are, especially with electronics, occasional use will be better than simple storage. Just be clear if you are expecting them back, so there aren't misunderstandings when you do come home.

Obviously, people's situations do change and you might find your stuff is losing it's temporary home. Hopefully, you've kept in touch and they let you know what's happening in enough time for you to take some sort of action. You might try reaching out to other friends and family in the area to see if they can, at least, collect and store your things long enough for you to find somewhere else to keep them. Of course, they might offer to permanently store your stuff (or at least as long as you are traveling), or arrange for it to move into a storage locker. This last thing will be hard to manage from the road, since there are things to sign and money to pay. If you have a really good friend, they might set up a storage locker for you in their name.

Obviously, if you don't have a storage locker set up before you leave and need to find a new location for things you'd left behind, getting another friend or family to pick it up and store it might be the best option.

An ignorant person with a bad character is like an unarmed robber, but a learned person with a blog is a robber fully armed. - Mickey Kaus

Should You Blog?

You are about to set off on an amazing adventure. There will be fantastic things to see, wildlife, perhaps a little love story - you will tread where ancients walked and you want the whole world to follow along. Or, at least your mom.

Many travelers start a blog or website to share their travels, but not all of them. Some people still travel just for themselves, and don't share anything except around a campfire at night. There isn't a right way to handle this, and it's up to you how much you want to share about your travels.

Keeping up a regular blog while on the road is a commitment of time and energy, so make sure you know what you are getting into before you leave. If you want to maintain a website or channel while on the road, start while you are still doing your preparation. There will be a lot to write or talk about, and it will give you an idea of the amount of time you will need to invest to produce content while on the road.

One thing which is important and I can't over-stress - unless you are funding your trip through your blog (which is difficult but can be done) - don't let your blog or updates get in the way of your trip. It is *your* trip, and you should focus on enjoying it. Along the way, if you have the chance to share with others, then by all means do so. Your friends and family back home will appreciate it. But don't let the need to keep them updated force you to do things or go places (in search of wifi, for example) where you don't want to go, or miss out on something because you had to write and post an update.

Of course, if you *are* funding your trip through your blog, or using the blog and trip to raise money for a charity, then you will have to invest time into it. While it won't be as much time as a full time 'job,' you should set aside a minimum number of hours a week for 'work.' This is where knowing how much time you need to keep to a posting schedule in advance will be helpful. If you are posting once a week, a text and picture blog won't be a huge investment of time, but the same schedule for a video blog (I know, they're called vlogs) will require a lot more time.

Also, once you are on the road, you might find you need more time to write or produce content than you had while you were home. The road has a lot of distractions, and you will have to learn how to deal with them. Again, if you are traveling for your enjoyment, I suggestion allowing the distractions in. I mean, it is your trip, right?

Types of Blog

When I wrote this, there were two types of blog in common use. The first is a text based blog, which you read on the internet, and the second is a video blog (called a vlog) which is more like a short tv show about your trip.

Of the two, blogs are easier. There is a lot of software allowing you to write offline anywhere, and then post when you have wifi or internet access. Because they are text and pictures (and you can control the size of the images) the files are small as far as the amount of data you need to move to get them online. Even slow, terrible wifi will usually work.

Vlogs are video records of your trip and adventures. While they are more work, they are quickly gaining in popularity. Some text based blogs are starting to add video content to improve the experience for their visitors. Filming and editing video does take more time than writing and taking pictures, and faster internet speeds (or more data on a mobile plan) are needed due to the increased size of the files needing upload. On the positive side, you don't have to worry about your spelling. Most vlogs are a combination of footage and voiceover, with some music added. How long each should be will depend on the content and audience, but as a viewer of many such videos let me just say 20 minutes of unedited helmet cam with the sound of the engine as the soundtrack is just not as interesting as you think it might be.

A third option is a podcast - there used to be a few of these but they seem to have all disappeared so I don't think anyone is doing them anymore. I think the basic problem with the format is that travel is, basically, a visual event and it's hard to capture that in audio for today's visual audience.

You can also post regularly to any number of online forums. For motorcycles, sites like ADVRider are full of people documenting their travels. Horizons Unlimited and model-specific forums are also places you can post, if they have an interest in that sort of thing. These posts can either drive traffic to your website, or be the sole online record of your trip (though going back and finding an old trip, especially on a forum with the volume ADVRider has, can be a struggle).

There is one more online-documentation option - Facebook. Yeah, I know, social media and all that, but if you want your story to be seen by more than just a few family and friends, you are going to have to learn how to work social media. And, Facebook has an option called a page. This is independent of your profile, so you can still post and share things with your friends which people following your trip won't see. You can post locations, pictures, and comments on the page, and with tags make the page findable by people looking to follow someone's adventure.

Choosing the Right One

So you are going to do some sort of online documentation of your trip. Cool.

Unless you will be just posting to Facebook - in which case you can skip most of this section - there are some things you should do. The first is get a URL. This is the special website name (like my travel blog Traveling250.com) you can give people when they hear about your trip and want to follow along. You don't *have* to buy a URL, if you want to save money on the whole process. When you set up a blog somewhere, it will come with a URL, but that URL will be a little more cumbersome than a custom one you choose for yourself. Put some thought into what you want this to be, but you can always choose something like your name - which will probably make your parents happy. You will have to 'buy' the URL, usually for a year at a time, though many hosting companies include a URL in their hosting package.

What is hosting?

When you post things online, they are actually on a computer somewhere (called a server, if you're curious and didn't know). When someone goes to your URL, they are actually using the internet to visit that server and look at the stuff you put there. Since building and maintaining servers is work, not to mention actually buying the computer and space in a building to put it, you generally have to pay for hosting.

Companies offer all kinds of different plans, but I recommend going with a company that has been around for a while, and a simple, basic plan (with a URL, if that's an option). You can also buy a URL on your own - if you're worried about future ownership - and then set things to point it at your server (which can be a little more complicated, so if you're worried about all this computer-stuff, just buy everything in one place).

If you don't want to spend the money on hosting (it can get expensive if you aren't careful about the options, but it doesn't have to be), there are free blog options. Squarespace, Blogger and Wordpress (which is the one I use) are options which don't charge you anything, but may put ads on your blog to try and earn some money off your viewers.

Hey, it's not like *you* gave them any money, and as I said - buying and maintaining the servers is someone's job.

To keep the costs down, I'd suggest getting a URL from somewhere, and then starting a free blog. The free blogs come with a URL related to the hosting service. So, my travel blog on wordpress is actually traveling250.wordpress.com. However, I give people Traveling250.com, and if you type that into a browser it takes you to my site. The text on the top even reads Traveling250, without any mention of Wordpress, except at the bottom on the page (that's called masking, by the way). I pay every year for the URL (It's usually around $5 for the year), and the blog doesn't cost me anything. Since it's a free site, I don't have as much control over the content as

I would if I'd hosted the blog somewhere (which could also be powered by Wordpress, but a much more technically complex version, allowing me to have more control over how things look and work). But it's more than enough for me to share images, words, and video from my trip, so it's what I use.

I had mentioned Facebook earlier. You don't have to pay anything for "hosting" there - it works like any other free blog and hopes to earn money from your visitors. You can also get a custom Facebook URL extension - which goes after Facebook.com (so mine is www.Facebook.com/GoingSmall).

I know some of you are thinking about YouTube. If you are sharing video content, that is the place to share it. And, assuming you've looked into this at all, you know that YouTube doesn't charge you to post content on their site. You can also monetize videos on YouTube and earn some money - which is nice. YouTube does like it when you have a separate site, though. That also allows you to post non-video content, like if you are planning a trip and want to share when you are going to be at certain locations so your fans can meet you. That sort of thing just works better as a site, rather than a video. Having a site also gives you that custom URL, which is easier to share with other people, and you can link to the videos from your "main" site.

So how often should you be posting? Well, that is completely up to you, but on the internet Content is King. Make sure whatever you are posting has a level of quality you're comfortable with. People don't bother with stuff that sucks. And, if you are traveling, it has to be a schedule you can maintain while on the road. This is where starting to post before you start traveling can help, as it will let you change your schedule from time to time, and get a sense of how long (for example) editing a video will take. Also, be prepared to work ahead, scheduling posts to happen when you aren't connected. This is especially useful for text/pic blogs, since they require less work (which isn't to say they don't take time) and you can upload a couple weeks worth of posts at a time, especially before going somewhere you won't have reliable internet.

Also, you don't have to limit yourself to one format. Feel free to write a blog, post videos, and do a Facebook page if you have the time, energy, and want to. Just remember that the trip is the what you are supposed to be on - not the internet.

Gear and Equipment

I'm not a big equipment guy; I think that people are a little bit shocked by that. I really don't care about gear in general. I care about people and their intentions to make music - it doesn't matter what equipment you have. - Dave Sitek

Vehicle Stuff

For me, adventures are a vehicle for traveling deep into the fabric of society, coming to know the environmental conditions that shape people's lives and viewing the present in the context of history. - Tim Cope

Oil And Tires

It's going to come up at some point, so let me address it as early as appropriate. Oil and tires.

If you go online to a forum for any vehicle you choose - and I really mean any of them - and ask about what tires you should use or what oil is best, you are going to get a lot of opinions. About the only place I haven't seen this turn into a massive argument is on the Prius forums, and even then people disagree.

On motorcycle or expedition vehicle forums, the topic is much more hotly debated. People with hundreds of thousands of miles and years of politely dealing with locals and their customs will defend what they think is best (or better) and condemn with great vehemence what they think is junk. They will utter dire warnings to any who even considers using anything other than what they recommend, which would be fine if there weren't three or thirty other people with just as strong a resume and completely different opinions. It's actually all rather confusing, and can be intimidating to anyone trying to just get this basic question answered.

Well, I am going to try and answer it.

What sort of oil and tires should you use? Let's talk about the oil first. Since you will need to change it, and probably more often than you are changing tires, you are eventually going to have to use whatever is available. Fancy, expensive blends with magical additives aren't going to be around once you get into developing countries, or even in developed countries if you are in smaller towns. So, don't bother. Find out what weight of oil is recommended for your engine and *try* to find and use that. If you can't, then get something close. It's better to have the right weight than the "other number," so if you are supposed to use 10w then make sure you are using 10w. Don't skimp on the oil changes - when it's time to change it then change it. If you aren't sure about the oil you used, or if you just don't like the available options, then you *can* wait a little while - but don't - *don't* -push your oil much further than you are supposed to. It's true that modern oils hold up much better than they did fifteen or twenty years ago, but there is still a lot going on inside those engines and when the oil stops doing its part things will go very, very wrong very, very quickly.

But don't stress on the oil too much (despite what I just said). Every engine needs oil, and so there will be oil available everywhere there are engines in use locally. Clean, almost right oil is better than expensive used-up oil. And, you can always change it again. Or, maybe you'll learn that your engine actually runs better on that odd, off brand stuff, and next time you're in a forum and someone asks about oil you can offer your opinion as well.

With that opinion on oil you might be able to guess my opinion on tires.

You probably have tires already installed, so start with those. Learn what they do well, and where they struggle, and if you find they struggle more than not, next time find something else - depending. Now, all tires struggle in mud except for mud-specific tires, and those are awful everywhere else so don't use that as a guideline. Also, generally speaking (by which I mean there are few exceptions) tires which are intended for off-road use will wear out faster than ones intended for street use. Some of them much faster, like less than 3,000 miles. That would work out to a lot of tire changes if those were your tire of choice, and there is no guarantee you will find replacements every time you need one. This is on the list of reasons why you see overland motorcycles carrying tires around with them. Other reasons are odd tires sizes, or wanting true off-road tires for when they go off-road, and wanting road tires for when they are on pavement.

Personally that seems like a lot more work, but I understand why they do it.

Many tires are described as "off-road" or some sort of "touring." In between these there are blended tires, usually referred to in some sort of fraction - "70/30" or "50/50," which is supposed to be a guide to how the tire is intended to be used. 70% on road and 30% off, for example. It could also be 70% off-road and 30% on, the order isn't important but the good news is tires meant to be off-road have a certain look, and it's not usually hard to figure out what the percentage is supposed to mean.

So, you need a set of tires. You didn't like how the bike handled on that one gravely road, so you decide you want a little more off-road in your tire. So, when you are at the shop and looking at the tires, mention you want something a little more off road capable. A good shop will know what you have and what you should go to, but with some experience you will be able to look at what is on the rack and pick out something.

Ah, experience. So easy to say "with experience" when the point of this whole book is that you don't have as much as you'd like. Well, in this case, just get some tires and see how they do. If you remember all those tires being suggested online and see one of those, give it a try. If not, try something that looks similar. Or, just take what they have in your size and be content. My point is that you shouldn't limit yourself - or worry too much about it before you even leave home. You are going to occasionally get crappy tires, and you are going to, more often than you think, have surprisingly good tires. But so long as you *have* tires you're in good shape.

Choosing a ride

Happiness is not something you postpone for the future; it is something you design for the present. - Jim Rohn

Motorcycle

I love motorcycles. It's still my preferred method of travel. It's not always the most comfortable. There are times it's the hardest thing in the world to get up, pack everything into a few small bags and throw a leg over the motorcycle for another day of noise and buffeting.

But you're so open on a motorcycle. So *exposed*. People see this and react. They smile when you take off your helmet and run a hand through helmet hair then try to wipe the dirt off your face. Motorcycles allow a connection with the rest of the world that larger vehicles just can't match.

So, if you are looking to take a long, overland trip on a motorcycle, what does that motorcycle need to have?

I have a confession. I think any motorcycle can do an overland trip. I know there are 'adventure' bikes, and I know they represent a large market share - with a matching large aftermarket of stuff it seems like you just *must* have if you want to ride much further than the nearest coffee shop. But I also think most of that stuff (including a special adventure bike) isn't *needed* for a long trip.

Having admitted that, there are some things that will make your trip *easier* if you have them. They aren't required, about all that you really need are two wheels and a motor (though given the number of people traveling on bicycles, I'm not sure you really *need* the motor). There are some things you should, however, think about when you are deciding on the motorcycle to bring on your trip.

Fuel range. There is a lot of stuff out there about how much range you *really* need to travel the world. Most people seem to go with "more is better." This is true, up to a point, but fuel costs money and adds weight - and on most motorcycles that weight is high up, which will make the bike harder to handle. And, if you have *more* range than you need, you are carrying that weight (not to mention any costs associated with aftermarket tanks) for nothing.

So how much range do you really need? If you are traveling as many overlanders do - which is to say regularly spending time in towns or traveling in areas where there are people and only occasionally going remote - then you can get by with 150-175 miles of range on a tank. If you are planning to do a lot more remote riding, where you might not see a vehicle or person for days and days (just so you know, this is getting increasingly hard to manage), then you should look to stretch your range as far as you can. Even with the 150-175 mile range, there will be times you won't have enough fuel to get to the next refill. That is okay, since those are the times you figure out a way to *temporarily* carry extra fuel, just for that section. Again, this is only occasional, so there's no need to permanently add that extra range, with the increased weight and cost.

Your motorcycle will also have to be comfortable for long distances over a variety of surfaces. I have a friend who loves cruisers - that laid back seating position. But, when riding on things other than smooth pavement, it's uncomfortable (since all the bumps go right to his back). So, when traveling overland, he uses a different motorcycle with a more standard seating position (where his feet are under his hips, and able to take some of the shock). This will be a personal choice for you, the rider, but take some trips on your motorcycle and try riding on some different surfaces just to see how it feels. Even if you are planning to stay on pavement for your whole trip, construction happens.

You will also need somewhere to put stuff. Even if you are traveling super light, carrying a toothbrush and change of underwear is nice. Many motorcycles come with luggage and, unless you have a really good reason to change them, you should use those (since you already have them, and don't have to buy anything else). If you do need to buy luggage, get the smallest size you think you can get away with. The larger the luggage you buy, the more stuff you will find to fill that space, even when you don't need the extra things you are trying to bring along. Eventually you will get tired of carrying them and send them home, but if you limit you space at the start, it will help you cut back on what you bring with to the essentials.

Truck

I titled this section "truck," but really mean anything that has about four wheels and a degree of off-road ability. I don't mean RVs or other large, self contained vehicles which are intended for good roads, but don't mean to exclude some pretty capable non-trucks which can be used for extended overland travel.

As I've mentioned elsewhere, I like traveling by motorcycle - but that isn't the same as not having traveled in something larger. And I fully understand some of the advantages (and disadvantages) of having more than two wheels.

So, you want to travel in a nice 4x4, get some dirt on the tires, see some stuff. One thing I am going to be honest up front about is that I am talking about Overland Travel - not extreme trail or "adventure" type driving. There are a ton of books about that already, and to be perfectly honest they are a very different sort of trip. Yes, you can take something set up for travel off road, and on trails, but it will never be as capable as something set up *just* to handle those trails - just as an "adventure motorcycle" can't be as good off-road as a trials bike. If you have doubts about this, go look at some hill climb videos and wonder why there aren't more Land Rovers, or anything with a roof tent.

So, why choose something other than a motorcycle? Well, as I've mentioned when giving budgeting classes, larger vehicles have one huge advantage over motorcycles - they don't have to move around as much. While they don't get as good MPG as a motorcycle, much of the other operating costs are similar or even better (ask a motorcyclist about tire costs and lifetimes). Since it's possible to carry more food and water, that means it's possible to find a nice spot and stay put for a while. This is a huge advantage over a motorcycle, which has limited space for supplies. They can also be more comfortable (since they are enclosed - it's nice sometimes to just turn up the heat a little when going over a pass, rather than wondering if you should stop and add layers before riding up, and then take them off, or just be cold for a while). When parking they also offer an increased feeling of security over a motorcycle (I've never had anything taken off my bike, but I've never had anything taken from my truck either), though finding parking can be more of a challenge.

The downsides? Well, if you are getting one of those cool expedition vehicles, the cost can be prohibitive. Naturally, motorcycles aren't free either, but the cost of a larger ride (even spread out over a long trip) adds up. To make it cost-effective, you have to be more aware of what you are spending money on, and what you are getting for that money.

Of course, apart from being able to stay put longer in a truck, I've found I am more willing to stay in some places than I would be in a tent. Perhaps I am not as trusting as I would like to be, but there is also light and noise issues which disappear when you can close and lock doors. While I try very hard to find free camping when traveling on a motorcycle, I often have to travel far off course, or adjust my basic route, for it to work. Free overnight parking for vehicles which lock are far more common, though they aren't always scenic. With a bit of research, you can find some really nice wild parking spots which don't allow "camping," and wouldn't work for anything you can't sleep in. And, if you are willing to spend a little, the options for urban parking (staying in cities is usually where most of my lodging costs go traveling on a bike, since "free" camping in a city might get me arrested) open up amazing possibilities. I overnighted once within a hundred yards of the horseshoe at Niagara Falls for $20 a night - a hotel which overlooks the view cost more than 10 times that much, and was a longer walk to get there besides.

There are parking downsides. Through central and south America, finding secure, off-street parking for a motorcycle was simple. Many places, especially in smaller towns, just had you roll it into their lobby, interior courtyard, or even your room. With a truck this doesn't work as well, and if you want secure parking (where you can leave your vehicle for a while without worrying about it) you will be more limited on where you can stay. Or, you can pay separately for parking, and accept not having perfect access to your stuff (depending on the availability and location of the parking).

So, there are good and bad things. Trucks have some advantages in comfort and when remote, being able to carry more supplies and more secure in the wilderness, while motorcycles have less upfront costs and handle urban and developed areas more easily. It's not that simple, obviously, and I don't want anyone thinking "I want to be more remote, so I'm going to get a truck because I read that in a book," and it's far more important to go and be on the road, rather than stress over the *how*.

Besides, motorcycles are more fun off road.

RV or Similar

I know when I think about RVs, I think of those large converted buses, 35-40ft long, with 3 TVs inside, and 2 outside. Of course, that is only a percentage of *actual* RVs, and some actually blend in with any other traffic on the road.

First, a quick overview. Those bus-like RVs are called Class A, and they are on bus chassis (which is why they look like buses). They tend to have the most space inside, as well as being the largest (obviously). Class B RVs are on van chassis, and can look just like a regular old van, but have all the stuff inside you would expect of a rolling home (like a toilet and shower, for example). There is a subgroup of these called B+ RVs, which are a newer type (so there aren't a lot of cheap used ones around). They are on a van chassis, but with a larger box on the back so they have more living space (more like a class C). And then there are the Class Cs - these are on truck chassis and have the distinctive bed-over-cab thing. More roomy than a class B, not as expensive as a class A, these usually have the bonus that some regular automotive garages will work on them (this varies almost based on who is working in the shop when you call, but being too long to too heavy won't work in your favor).

I split off RVs from trucks because of two distinct differences. First, few RVs (usually specialized class B models) are capable off road. The larger ones are only barely able to drive *on* road (straight roads are your friend), and seem intended to move from one RV park to another. Second, there is little that is subtle or inconspicuous about an RV. You aren't going to hide one anywhere, and if they are much larger than a regular vehicle you are going to have issues finding parking for them.

Most RV travelers get around some of these limitations by using a towed vehicle. They find somewhere to park the RV, and then travel locally with the smaller vehicle. While this works great in developed countries (particularly the USA, where I think they came up with the idea), as a long term overland travel option it has limits.

This might sound all pretty bad, and we haven't even talk about the cost (which actually isn't much worse than the truck section, especially if you are willing to buy used), but there are good things about RV travel. No matter how comfortable you get your expedition equipped 4x4, you aren't going to compete with a true RV. The full sized bed with real mattress, full kitchen, fridge and freezer. Even having a "real" bathroom is a level of decadent luxury you don't realize how badly you've missed until you have it again. Depending on what sort of RV you use, camping can be a simple matter of pulling into a spot, turning off the engine, perhaps hitting a switch or two, and you're all done. No set up, no take down, no unfolding of anything. If it's raining, you sit on the couch. If it's cold, you turn up the heat. The end.

That might sound pretty nice, but I am not a fan of the attendant isolation. If you never have to go outside, it becomes very easy to *never go outside*. Where is the fun in that? Of course, I also enjoy freshly baked cookies, so I guess it's all a compromise.

Bicycle

I am going to say this right up front. I have huge respect for people who are doing long term travel on a bicycle. Of all the options listed here, this is the only one I don't have any personal experience with. Mostly, I admit, because the idea of pedaling up a mountain seems like a lot of work, without also bringing along everything I need to live. I do want to *try* it someday, but in the mean time I really appreciate having a motor for mountains and limit my pedaling to flatter terrain.

Bicycles have many of the *space* restrictions of motorcycles, with the added issue of severe *weight* requirements. While you can carry and extra 20 pounds on a motorcycle and get away with it, even if the bicycle frame can support those extra 20lbs (and they probably can, RTW bicycles are incredibly durable), *you* will have to provide the energy to move that extra 20lbs while you travel. For this reason, even though they (technically)have more *space*, most bicyclist's kit looks more like that of a backpacker - small, lightweight, and extremely minimal.

That might not sound great - manual labor and few comforts - but pedaling your way around the world is just about as inexpensive as it gets. Even if you spend a *lot* on your bike and gear, you won't be close to what someone with a motor spends (unless they went really cheap, which means you will have nicer equipment). Shipping across oceans is much, much easier (most airlines take your bike as checked luggage - there is a fee but it's nothing compared to the cost of shipping a vehicle). There are no import duties (usually), no fuel, no registration or insurance.

The pace of travel is much slower, allowing you to take in the world to a much greater extent than other travelers. Of course, distances become further. I remember meeting a pedaler in Chicken Alaska with a split rim on his wheel. He needed to get about 60 miles to get it fixed, which isn't that far with an engine to push you along. It was more than a day's travel time for him though, so he was looking for a truck to give him a ride.

I was on a motorcycle, so there wasn't room for him and his bike.

Creeping along with pedal power is also much, *much* quieter. Just about every bicyclist I've met has stories from getting close to wildlife (sometimes too close), since there isn't the usual noise to scare them away (or at least alert them to you being there).

The pace does have its downsides. I often comment to motorcyclists that, if the weather is too cold for riding, all they have to do is ride somewhere warmer. Bicyclists are more limited, since they can't cover the same distances as quickly, and so have to be more aware of the seasons and expected weather where they are, and where they are going.

RTW Ticket

I mention the RTW ticket because I think it's a cool idea, but this is really a section for the backpackers.

If you haven't heard about a RTW ticket, it's actually a series of plane tickets which you buy all at once. The cost is dependent on the number of "legs," and limited by the start and end needing to be at the same place. Each leg ends somewhere, and a certain period of time later (weeks or months) the next leg leaves from the same airport and flies to the next city.

Repeat.

So, you arrive in, say, Quito in Ecuador. In 7 weeks, you have a flight out of Ecuador to, maybe Buenos Aires (it's really up to you where a RTW ticket will take you). So, during those 7 weeks, you get to explore Ecuador, using whatever transport you arrange locally (or your bicycle, if you brought it along, but I think it's more common to use public transport).

Since you are dependent on local transport when you aren't flying, its usually best to travel with a single backpack, rather than suitcases or multiple bags. Something small enough to be a carry on for flights is even better, since it greatly reduces the risk it doesn't arrive in your next city after a flight. This means you will have to cut way back on what you are carrying from destination to destination, but since you (probably) won't be cooking or camping, and won't have a vehicle to maintain, you should be able to limit what you bring with. Remember you can always get items locally as needed, so don't be afraid to travel light.

The cost for such a trip will vary considerably depending on the things you do along the way, but the tickets should be around $10,000USD - and can less or more depending where you go and how long you stop. I recently priced out a route that was only about $4,000 a person, giving about a week in various cities I wanted to visit (which isn't a lot of time to see the countries the cities are in, obviously, and only a taste of the city). This doesn't include food, lodging, local travel, or any other expenses you might find along the way, but as you can see it's possible to take one of these trips without spending much, about what you might pay for a vehicle for one of the more "standard" overlanding options. Of course, with a RTW you don't have the vehicle, and whether this is a positive thing is a matter of personal choice. Remember - all that matters is that you *are traveling,* not how you are going about it.

Perfection is not attainable, but if we chase perfection we can catch excellence. - Vince Lombardi

Carrying Food / Water

I think that traveling makes anyone a bit of a foodie. Eating and food are a large part of any local culture, and most travelers I know are on the road to experience those cultures (as well as the places) as deeply as possible. That means eating.

But many travelers are also on the road to experience places rarely visited, perhaps never visited, and even if you are only hopping town to town, there are going to be times when you will want to make your own meals. If you are traveling in developed countries then preparing your own meals becomes a huge budget saver - restaurants are expensive all over but in developed countries the cost *feels* higher, due to the higher cost of living and (usually) less favorable exchange rates.

So, you want to carry food. You should also, always, be carrying water. Humans can live for quite a while without food (though it's not very pleasant), but our bodies will shut down and die very quickly without water. And I mean *water*, not energy drinks, coffee, or soda.

Let talk about the water first, since it's more important. Despite being important, it's a pain to carry. Awkward and heavy and it needs special containers. How much you need will vary some depending on the climate and how you personally go through it (people to vary some on how much water they need daily). Those special containers will also continue to add bulk to your luggage even after you've consumed the water they were carrying.

There is also the issue of getting fresh water while traveling, but I'll cover that later.

So, how to carry water. Hard metal or plastic containers are probably the least expensive, and both are quite durable. Both, however, won't get smaller as you drink the water, and both are at risk of developing leaks if carried in such a way they rub against things or if you happen to crash onto them.

Another option are soft bladders. These are newer technology - though they aren't really "new" anymore. They come in more sizes than hard containers and get smaller as you empty them, which is nice for packing. I use a soft container in the form of a hydration pack in my backpack. It holds around 3 liters of water, which is enough pure water for a couple days under normal conditions (I also usually have other drinks, but be careful about caffeine, since those drinks are usually dehydrating). It's also nice since it allows me to drink while riding, preventing dehydration without having to stop and get off the bike everything time I want something (or, worse, only drink when I stop for something else. That never ends up being enough).

If you want a soft bladder but don't want to wear a backpack (and don't want to spend the money for a soft bladder, they aren't cheap), buy a box of wine. Yes, a box of wine, you don't have to drink it. Or have some friends over and let them drink it, doesn't matter. But inside that box is a soft plastic bladder, and that bladder (once you rinse it out a few times) makes an excellent water carrier.

If that's where you are carrying your water, let's think about where you are carrying your food. On my motorcycle I carry all my food in my tank bag. I know most riders keep a bunch of little random stuff in there, but using the tank bag just for my food means it's very easy to remove and secure, when I'm in places where food security is an issue (like when there are bear - but raccoons and smaller critters can be a problem too). It also means all my food smells are kept away from my camping gear and clothes, another bonus for those areas where you have to worry about what might come walking through your site at night.

If you are in a hard-sided vehicle (like a car or truck), you can be a little more relaxed about food, but not much more. In some places it's still a good idea to store food away from your camp, and keeping the smell of food away from clothes and camping gear is always a good idea. Use containers that seal tightly and don't leave things out when you are done cooking. Also, try to wash up right away - the sooner nothing smells like it might be worth checking out the better chance no one uninvited appears for dinner.

Tools

The most important tool you should have with while you are traveling is a printed copy of the *service* manual for your vehicle. Yes, I know they're bulky and expensive, but if you break down somewhere - seriously break down - you are going to need that manual and you might not be able to print it where ever you happen to be. And yes, I know you can have a digital copy stored, but if you leave your motorcycle or truck with a local mechanic *they* are going to need that manual. You probably won't want to also leave your computer or tablet with them while your bike is being fixed. Even if they don't understand the language the manual is in, they will still have the pictures and various numbers and values listed - and that is the stuff they really need.

The next things you should carry in your tool kit are the things you need for flat tires. These will vary a little depending on the types of tires you have (tube or tubeless) and the vehicle you are traveling with, but motorcyclists should at least have a set of tire irons (I use two, many people say three is better), replacement tube, and compressor. Preferably the compressor will run on 12v, so you can use the vehicle to power it, but a battery one is better than nothing. Now, for those of you who are thinking "I have tubeless tires and don't need that stuff," the truth is you do. If you are going off road, though it can happen on pavement as well (especially in Alaska, which I swear uses ground up razors for their roads), you can so damage a tire that those little gummy worms aren't going to seal the hole (or tear). Which means you need to get the tire off and put a tube in, until you can get a new tire. So, carry the gummies for simple punctures and save the irons and tubes for the serious stuff. Also, for your tubeless tires, you will want some of those CO2 canisters for reseating the bead. Again, don't *just* carry those - have a compressor and use *that* for all the "normal" flats you get along the way. But if you need to reseat your tire's bead, you are going to need much, much higher pressures than most small compressors can manage.

So, yeah. If you have tubeless tires you will probably want to have more stuff in your "deal with a flat" kit. If it makes you feel better, when you get to just use a gummy and get back on the road, those of us with tube tires will be very jealous.

Once you have those two things (service manual and tire repair), the rest of your kit should be focused on whatever you need to do the regular maintenance on your vehicle - whatever that vehicle is and whatever maintenance you are planning to handle yourself while on the road. You should be trying as many of those task as you can before leaving, so you know what you'll need and be familiar with the process before you even get on the road. While practicing, you should be using a tool kit dedicated to the vehicle. **Don't Skimp.** If you use it, it goes with the vehicle and get another one for home, or get one for the vehicle the next chance you have and put it in the bag. Be careful about over doing it. If you need one or two sockets, then just include the one or two sockets - not the whole set. It you are too OCD to split up a set like that (I admit, it's a struggle for me), go to the hardware store and just get the ones you need. Or buy a set just to break up, which might cost less than individual sockets, and maybe you'll feel better if that was the plan all along.

With the maintenance tools out of the way, you're done. Stop packing tools.

No, really - stop.

Okay - I know you bought that one thing that is really cool and you really want to bring it along, but you know you probably won't use it - unless it's for maintenance or flats, in which case you should already be packing it - so you don't *need* it, you just *want* it. If that's the case but you really feel like you have to have it along, go ahead and pack it, but understand *why* you are packing it.

There is one last set of tools you should think about having. Well, tools and parts. I didn't mention parts because I don't think you should carry a lot, or any at all, along with you. For every story I've heard about someone breaking down and having just the thing they needed, I've heard a couple dozen from people who carry a collection of parts which are never the ones they need. Or nothing breaks at all.

Things will probably break. When they do, help will appear to get you back on the road.

Motorcycle Luggage

As I mentioned elsewhere, you need luggage for your motorcycle (unless you aren't bringing anything along with you on the road, I guess). Most adventure motorcycles now come with hard metal bags, at least as an option, and other touring motorcycles might have plastic or metal luggage. But there are a lot, the vast majority, of motorcycles that don't have luggage at all.

So, if you need luggage, what sort of luggage do you need? I will say right up front that I prefer soft luggage to hard. It's more flexible, less expensive, easier to repair, and less likely to cause injuries in case of a fall. Yes, I said cause injury in a fall. I know a lot of riders credit their hard luggage for protecting their leg when they fell over, but I also know a lot of riders with knee and leg injuries and fractures from their legs hitting those same bags when they fell. So, clearly there are good and bad things. If you decide you want hard bags get smaller ones that don't extend too far forward.

And speaking of size, just get the smallest bags you think you can get away with in the first place. While you will find things to stick in your luggage if you have extra space, if your space is limited you will make better decisions about what to bring with while traveling. If you do end up not having enough room, look at adding a bag (perhaps another tail bag or larger tank bag) rather than upgrading everything and having too much room. Ricing around overloaded will cause you more issues than having to carry one extra bag will. Also, when you reduce what you are carrying (which you probably will), removing that extra bag will be easier than downsizing all your luggage.

Soft bags don't provide as much physical protection from impacts, but things inside them don't rattle around as much as things do in hard luggage. Since my luggage isn't usually full, having soft bags means I can make the bags smaller, while hard bags are the same size all the time. If you have hard bags, try to pack fragile things in softer items to provide some cushioning - and I include tools as "fragile items," since they can damage other things in the luggage, or the luggage itself.

Odds are pretty good your side bags are going to have some abuse while you are on the road. Soft bags will pick up scuffs or tears, hard luggage scuffs and dents. Soft bags are usually repairable with a needle and thread, and some time, but if you have to repair hard luggage you will likely need a shop or garage with rivets and/or welding materials (assuming you can't just pound everything back into shape). If you do need welding, know that some of the fancier hard bags (made of alloys so they are lighter and (in theory) more damage resistant) will need special welding rods to be welded. Some garages will also be less excited about welding odd materials (it was a problem with aluminum for years, but more people are working with it now, especially in urban environments) so you might be stuck using a hammer and finding a waterproof liner.

Soft luggage also provides a huge cost savings over hard luggage. It really isn't much of a comparison, since the cost of one hard side bag usually covers the cost of a full set of soft luggage. If you are looking at factory options, make sure you do some research and work out if those bags are the best value for your money. While you might have to get the factory luggage to get other options you want, still take some time and see what else is available - and remember to look at *smaller* bags, rather than larger ones.

Soft luggage also has *two* advantages in the area of weight. Well, one and a half. They weigh less than metal or plastic hard bags, or should unless the fabric is really heavy or the metal incredibly light. Hard luggage also requires a rack, which adds weight to the rear of the bike was well. Soft luggage *might* require a rack, which would also add weight, but there are also soft bags which drape over the rear seat of the motorcycle. While you might think I'd meant the lack of a rack was the advantage, but really I mean that putting the bags over the rear seat puts the weight of the bags *on the rear seat*, which is where motorcycles are designed to carry weight, rather than on racks (which actually pull out at the frame rather than down on the suspension).

Security is also a consideration for luggage, and (after the crash protection) frequently given as a reason to get hard bags instead of soft. Personally, I've never had anything taken off my motorcycle, and have used soft bags for most of my traveling. There are security nets and similar options for adding security to soft bags, but if you just aren't comfortable without locks, then get hard luggage and locks (just remember the other things I said - materials, cost, size - when you're shopping).

Lastly, but importantly, if you already have luggage on your motorcycle, just use that luggage. Don't spend money you could use for actually going places on replacing something you already have, unless there is a really good reason to (like a test pack shows you the luggage simply won't work, or it's broken). Go and travel, have fun, see things, and if it really doesn't work then change it for the next time.

Mobile Power

If you are traveling with a lot of extra stuff - I mean extra stuff that requires electrical power - then you are going to eventually run into the need to keep it all charged or powered.

In a way, being primarily a motorcycle traveler is an advantage in this area. Since I can only carry so much food and water, I need to move occasionally to resupply. While the engine is running, the motorcycle is making more electricity than it needs and I use the extra to recharge the battery. Then I can use the battery to recharge everything else (usually no more than my phone and a Bluetooth system on my helmet).

Now, if you are traveling with something larger than a motorcycle, and not carrying too much more in the way of electronics (maybe a tablet and camera), then you are in good shape as far as keeping things charged. If you don't have an engine, or if you are looking to keep a lot more stuff in power (I'm looking at you, truck guys with the fridge), then you should be looking at alternatives.

Since I already called out truck people, I'll start there. While keeping something like a laptop charged shouldn't be much of a problem, keeping the fridge running for a week while you are sitting in one place might be. Even with the efficiency of modern compact fridge/freezer systems, you are going to want to add a second electrical system (usually a second battery, outlets and perhaps an inverter, and a way to recharge the battery from the engine or external source without it draining the battery connected to the engine). I know there was a lot in that sentence, so I'll explain further. If you are planning to run a lot of electrical items while camped, or a couple higher drain items, you are going to want those things to use a *different* electrical system than the one that starts the engine - i.e. the one that your truck came with. This new electrical system will need one or more batteries. It will also need ways to plug in the things you want to power. If you are looking to recharge your laptop, you will need an inverter, which will change the electricity in the battery to the kind you get from wall outlets (I know this is a complicated subject, and I know some of you will know all this. Not all of you will, though, so bear with me). You will need a way to recharge those batteries, either from the engine (while running) or from something external. Plugging in at a campground, for example, or solar panels.

There are kits which do all this you can buy and install yourself. Or, you can go to a local shop and have them install something for you (somewhere that does custom sound systems will be the place to start). Or, you can reduce your electrical needs. Up to you.

Since I mentioned solar power, and earlier travelers without motors, these go together. You can get solar panels which will recharge your vehicle system, which are large but vehicle - portable. If you are on foot or a bicycle, you can get (much) smaller solar panel units which either charge a device directly or recharge smaller power packs, which you then use for recharging. Personally I like the power pack idea more. It does add complexity, it also allows power to be stored for times when you can't use solar.

And, yes, if you are on a motorcycle you can also use solar panels to keep things powered or charged. When I was still traveling with a computer, I used solar panels to power a 100w inverter, which I could plug my computer into. Eventually, I got tired of carrying the panel and inverter, and the computer for that matter, and left all of it behind. You always end up needing less than you start out with, and electrical gadgets (and the power to run then) isn't immune.

Non Vehicle Equipment

The biggest adventure you can take is to live the life of your dreams. - Oprah Winfrey

Taking Pictures

You probably got the idea to take a long trip from looking at pictures. I know many of us have read books, but no matter how great those books are (and some are really great), it's the pictures that capture our attention.

So, obviously, you will want to take pictures of *your* trip, either to share with family and friends, post online, or use to launch an awesome career as an author and speaker on overland travel (okay, this last scenario is trickier than it sounds). *What* you use to take the pictures doesn't matter as much as you think it would. If you speak with many photographers, they will tell you it's not the camera but the skill of the person using it.

That is, to a certain extent, crap - but not entirely.

Digital cameras have, and will continue to improve to an amazing extent. When digital SLR cameras were introduced, they had technical specs that wouldn't even make it into a cheap cell phone today. And (at least in the high end phones), cell phone cameras have reached the point where it's sometimes hard to tell the difference between an image taken with a phone versus one taken with a $3,000 camera.

Having read that, you might be more confused over what camera you should use. If you can get that photographer to hold still, they will also tell you the best camera is the one you have with you. So you will want a camera that you are comfortable carrying and using. For me, that isn't a camera that costs as much as two months on the road. Especially when I don't need that much camera.

A few other things to think about.

If you are looking to print your images in a book (for example), you are going to want *at least* 8 megapixels. When I wrote this, you really have to go looking for a camera that has fewer, so don't stress over it too much. If you are hoping to *sell* your pictures to someone (magazines for example, usually as part of an article) you will want *at least* 12MP. A few years ago, print magazines were happy with 8MP, so I expect in a few more years they will want 14MP or more. This is the current level of most high end (but not camera focused) smart phones, so if you have a modern smartphone you might not even need to get a dedicated camaera.

Apart from MP, another thing which has a real impact on image quality is the size of the sensor. Phone cameras, since they have less space to spend on their camera, have a smaller sensor than just about every dedicated camera on the market. Larger sensors make for cleaner images, and other bonuses like richer colors and better performance in low-light.

Those might sound like good reasons for a dedicated camera, but there is a downside. A camera - really any camera, but the larger and more obvious it is, the more it's true - forms a barrier between you are the world. It removes you from a situation, a place, the people, and sets you apart from them, if even for a moment. It also changes how the people on the other side of the lens act, sometimes much differently than they were just a few seconds earlier. Cell phones, however, are everywhere. People are more comfortable with them, and it's not uncommon anymore for people to stop and take a quick photo of something, almost without thinking. That image might not be technically as clean as one taken with a high-end digital SLR, but just getting that SLR out might end the chance to get the image.

So what camera should you have? I have been happy with my cell phone (currently an iPhone 6S) for years. It has a 12MP camera and impressive image stabilization. A few years ago I got a Nikon D3300 DSLR, with 24MP, and there really is a difference between the images the two cameras capture. While the Nikon is small for a DSLR, it's clearly a camera, and it doesn't fit in my pocket. While traveling through South America I carried a small point and shoot Canon Elph. It was smaller than my phone (a Google Nexus at that time, 8MP) and had a larger sensor and more MP. With a spare battery I didn't even bother with multiple memory cards, just moving everything to a hard drive and online back up every few days, as internet service allowed.

And I think that should be your goal. A small, unobtrusive camera that you can easily carry with you as you are out and about, which takes a better image than your phone (otherwise, just use your phone), isn't prohibitively expensive, and you like to use. The catch is, thanks to continuing improvements in cell phone cameras, these small cameras are a vanishing species.

But there is more to modern media than still images. YouTube, Live on Facebook, and whatever comes out next. Video works well online. Better than pictures, as people's available bandwidth increases, but it's a lot more work - both to capture the video and to make it into something people will want to see.

As a quick aside - 40 minutes of uncut helmet cam footage might *seem* like a good idea, but it isn't. It really isn't.

Most dedicated cameras (and phone cameras) will capture HD video. Video takes a lot more memory than pictures, which means you will need storage for it while traveling and accept longer times to get the stuff backed up online. Getting the video edited can also take up a lot of time you might want to spend on other things (like doing stuff), but there is no question it's the best way to gain attention and a following for your trip, if that's what you are looking for.

Of course, if that *is* what you are looking for, then you should invest in a few things to make it easier. While most smart phones are capable of video editing and adding effects, unless you are working to show what you can do with just a phone while on the road, get a dedicated computer (or tablet) for your video editing. If nothing else, having somewhere to upload raw videos (to get them off whatever you are using to record) will be useful. As I mentioned, it's hard to get an idea of how much electronic memory video takes up until you've spent a few days filming, especially in HD quality.

Since I am fan of keeping things simple, most of my video is shot and edited on my phone, or occasionally a tablet if I've brought it with. I can't compete with higher end systems, and don't try. You have to decide how much money and time you want to invest.

Computers

The first question is whether or not you actually need to bring a full computer with while you are traveling. If you ask in an online forum you find it comes down to a matter of personal preference - which means no, you don't *need* to bring a full-on computer with while you are on the road - but that doesn't mean you don't want to.

First, work out what you are planning to use the computer for. Maybe you have a job where you will need to remote login for things or dedicated software. If so you will have definite requirements for anything you are traveling with.

If you are just planning to use the computer for things like social media, blogging, or other tasks, consider using a mobile device instead of a full computer. Large phones or smart tablets might be able to accomplish the same things you are trying to use the computer for, but at less cost. Many phones and tablets also have hard or protective cases available (since they are intended to be carried around, which means they get dropped from time to time), which will add some security to your electronics.

There are some things which, even now, mobile devices can't manage as well as full computers (though there are fewer and fewer things on this list as tablets take over the mobile computer market). You will have to decide for yourself if a mobile device meets your needs or not. It's usually better to try some shorter trips without other devices before committing to one thing or the other. Make sure you do, on those trip, everything you think you

126

will need to do once you are on the road "for real." Blogging, video editing, reading or entertainment, anything you can think of.

Once you know what you are carrying, you need to work out how to keep it safe while on the road. There are several hard cases available for full computers (most of them don't allow you to use the computer at the same time), some of which will fit inside motorcycle luggage. While I prefer soft bags, if you have a lot invested in your computer, having a piece of luggage which locks might make you more comfortable. Make sure your computer is fully powered off before riding anywhere. When in "sleep" or "stand-by" modes, computers will still spin up hard drives occasionally, and any severe bump or jarring could destroy it. With newer, SSD type drives this is less of a problem (mobile devices, obviously, can handle movement), but it's still a good idea to power everything off when you're done with it.

While we're on the issue of power, there is also the question of keeping everything charged while you're on the road. I have a section on mobile power later, but briefly - smaller, mobile electronics can be charged from the motorcycle while riding (assuming you can charge from a USB, there are plenty of 12v to USB adaptors around. Most gas stations have bins of them). Computers require a little more effort, since they run on household currents. Different countries use different voltages from the wall, and most of them are nice enough to also use different plugs (so you don't accidentally damage anything). Companies make the converters to whatever your home current happens to be (or to USB).

When I was traveling with a regular computer (I've switched to a tablet in the last few years - most of this book was written on one) I used a medium-sized solar panel to run a 100w inverter, which could then charge my computer. The computer, a small, inexpensive netbook, would run almost 10 hours on a full charge, which would work out to a couple days to a week of actual use, depending on how much I used it. Its primary function was to back up pictures, with some blog writing, which I can now do without the computer.

One other thing to consider while looking at your computer is how well it works with your other electronics. Apple products, for example, work very well together, but an android phone won't work as well with an apple computer. IPhones also struggle with some features when paired with a PC. Any issues will have to be found and worked out before you start on the road, because you aren't going to want to deal with them while traveling.

Looking back over this section, it sounds a lot like I'm telling you not to bring a computer with while you're traveling. I'm not, not really. If you have a computer and it does the things you need to do then use one while you travel - since that's better than buying something new (with money you could spend to travel). You don't need to bring a computer along with just to have one, and if do want to buy something specifically for travel then think about what you need to actually do and get what works best. In truth, many tablets are as expensive as laptops, so there is less savings there than you would expect.

Clothes

Everyone needs clothes. I mention, when giving a packing class, clothes and personal items are such a common thing to pack we rarely think about them. Going for a weekend? Throw some things in an overnight bag and call it done.

I traveled with rider on a two week trip, and they brought fresh clothes for just about every day. It was a lot of clothes. In the end, I don't think he wore them all.

No one has enough clothes to wear something clean every day. That is why we do laundry. When on a longer trip, say more than a long weekend, bringing with all the clothes you need for fresh things every day becomes too much to deal with. It's easier to just pack enough so that you don't have to do laundry constantly.

It's also not just how much you bring with, but what it is. While it's easy to say (you've probably heard it all the time) "dress in layers," that isn't really helpful when trying to work out what to pack for a long trip. So, I'll try to break it down a little.

First, some comments on materials. Actually, before that - when I talk about *packed* clothes, I am referring to the stuff in the luggage. In addition to that stuff, I have on (at a minimum) a t-shirt, underwear, and a pair of socks, I wear motorcycle pants when riding, and these also serve as my "pants" for short stops during the day. Everything else - I mean everything - is packed away on the bike. Even if, when it's time to leave and I need a liner or rain gear, I have to take it off the bike to put it on. This simple system will mean everything has a place while you're on the road (as opposed to having to cram things away later, or strap them to the outside of your luggage).

Now, materials. I like jeans, but I don't travel with them anymore. They are too heavy, and take too long to dry when they get wet (even damp). If I knew they would never get wet, I might be tempted, but I pack one pair of khaki-type pants. Recently I bought a pair of those fancy (expensive) synthetic pants, and they are extremely nice, but I'm not yet convinced they are worth the cost. While they might last longer than less expensive pants, they will be much harder to replace if needed while on the road. If you have them, then by all means use them - but I don't think you *need* them. I am more relaxed about shirts, and usually have three (wearing one, with two extra). Of course, for underwear I'm back to synthetic materials. It's all well and good to change shirts on the side of the road, but it's a different matter to change your drawers.

I want to say this again - if you are already traveling and have clothes that you like and are comfortable in, then use those. Everyone reading this owns clothes (I hope), so there isn't any reason to buy *new* things before traveling (that just spends money that would be better spent on the road). Those clothes will wear out, and when they do you can try a different material for the replacement. Or not, if you like what you're using.

So, what do I actually have packed? I am not a fan of packing lists, since I think everyone will have their own take on what they need, but this is everything I carry in my clothes section on the bike:

One pair of pants
One long sleeve shirt
One pair of thermal underwear (top and bottom)
One pair of shorts (for pjs or swim trunks, as needed)
Three pairs of socks
Three pairs of underwear
Two short sleeve t-shirts
One Towel

And that's it. Most of the time, with wearing things more than once, I can go a week or so between laundry. When it's really hot, that time gets shorter, since I get sweatier. This lines up with how often I like to have a hard roof, so it's perfect for me. As I said earlier, you might have different preferences. Just remember - it's okay to re-wear things and to do laundry while traveling. It's less okay to overpack, or to have that laundry be such a chore it takes most of a day to take care of.

Medications and Medical Supplies

Concern over medical emergencies while on the road is a common reason I hear from people talking themselves out of long term travel. I can't say *nothing* will happen, most of those things can also happen at home. It's all a matter of what you want to do with your time.

But, perhaps you are getting on the road and either want, or need, to bring medications or medical supplies along with. What, and how?

Well, if you are looking at general, over the counter type medications you might want to pack, I would suggest four.

The first is ibuprofen, or some sort of non-steroid anti-inflammatory (NSAID). When you are sore at the end of a day's riding, or hiking, or twisted an ankle or have any other sort of trauma-related pain, this is what you should be taking. Don't over do it, and unless you are repeatedly stressing yourself you should only need it for a few days at a time, but it can be very helpful when you need it.

The second is acetaminophen (Tylenol). While it is also a pain reliever (and you can take it along with the ibuprofen for those really bad aches), this is mostly for when you feel sick and have a fever. Fevers happen while traveling, and this will help keep them under control. Again, you should only need it for a few days - any longer and you might want to find some real medical attention (or just rest for a while, if you didn't when you developed the fever).

The third and fourth are related to "lower GI issues." Without being to explicit, you want something to get things going when they are stopped, and stop things when they are going too much. Again, stomach issues are common for travelers and this combination of medications will help with whichever variety you might (but hopefully don't) develop.

You should carry these medications in their original bottles, and definitely shouldn't mix them. More on that later.

If you need to take prescription medications, first of all - don't worry. You should be able to get the medications you need in most major cities, though in some instances you might need to see a local physician first. Outside the USA, most medical care and medications are inexpensive, so lacking insurance won't be as much of an issue as you might think. Of course, on a short trip you might want to talk to your doctor and just get enough of a supply to last you while you are on the road.

It is even more important that prescription medications be carried in their bottles, with the label intact. Don't mix the pills, and don't use those handy little trays, where you put some in each day. While it might never come up, while at a land border one of the officers could go through your things and they aren't going to want to see a bunch of random pills all mixed together. Even if you eventually sort it all out, it's an extra headache easily avoided by just bringing along the original bottles. If you have several bottles of the same medication (anti-malaria pills often come this way), you can combine them into one bottle so long as all the pills look the same. Even if they are the same but look different, the border guard looking into the bottle won't know that. He will just see more than one type of pill and want you to explain why.

If you have medications that require keeping cold (such as insulin), you will have to look into battery operated coolers. This need might also influence *what* you travel in, since some vehicles will make it easier than others. You can also talk to your doctor about options which aren't as temperature sensitive, but be willing to listen to what they say, even if it's something you don't want to hear.

One other piece of equipment many will want to carry is a first aid kit. Don't go too crazy on this - think about the things you commonly use at home and build a similar kit for yourself (think bandaids, lots of bandaids). While there are some pretty complex and "complete" seeming kits available, many contain things you will never need or use, taking up space and money that could be used to buy more of the things you will need and use. Getting one or two larger bandages (such as 8x7) might be recommended, if you have the room, but I generally only carry the smaller (4x4) ones (when I carry anything other than a selection of band-aids).

If you are carrying a dedicated first aid kit, make sure everyone you're traveling with knows where it is. This is also true for medications you might be carrying and would need in case of emergencies, such as inhalers or epi-pens. If you need one, and can't get it yourself, you will want someone to know where to go.

Other Things

I have a teddy bear. I'm not ashamed of it - his name is Blue and he is (by now) quite well traveled. He's large for a travel stuffed animal, almost 20 inches tall. He has a motorcycle jacket and (despite what I said about them in the clothes section) jeans. He's a little dirty, but cleans up when needed.

Actually, I got Blue from a Build-a-Bear shop. This meant he had access to a couple different clothing options and they re-stuff him when needed. It's been needed from time to time. He travels in my backpack, and comes out for pictures. When I use him as a road-side pillow he stays in the bag (which keeps him cleaner).

I know a lot of travelers who carry stuffed animals for pictures on the road, and while I mention mine (and theirs), this section isn't about them exactly. There are going to be things you want to bring with on your trip which don't automatically fit into any of the other sections I've listed.

It's okay, you can still bring them.

Another common travel item are books. I love reading, but books are bulky and hard to travel with (especially on a motorcycle where space is tight). I got around this by buying a Kindle, which held all the books (including guidebooks) I wanted while on the road. I spent the extra money to get a model with Amazon's Whispersync - which provided (free) unlimited internet. It was enough online access for email and looking up things on Wikipedia, which was all I really needed. Even while I was traveling WiFi was becoming more and more common, and I don't know if that service is needed anymore, but it certainly was useful for me. You can also pack actual, for real, printed books. Just about every hostel will have a book exchange, so when you finish what you're reading you can swap out for something new.

I hate giving up books, so I am not so good at book exchanges.

Other travelers carry other things. I know one who roasts his own coffee beans. Some carry small printers, so they can leave physical images behind on their travels. Others carry stickers or pens. After a couple test trips you will get a sense of what you might want to bring with on your longer travels. Work out how best to deal with any bulk or cost, preferably before you hit the road "for real."

Along with things you bring along with, there are also things you pick up along the way. No, I don't mean the book exchange books - but the rugs and mugs and small statues (and maybe large statues, who am I to judge?) while you are visiting foreign lands. Memories and even pictures are all well and good, but physical objects, perhaps made by local craftsmen, have a special place and power. They may also be the best way to directly support those cultures we travel to see (though I do understand how tourists can corrupt and destroy those cultures as well). You have to use your judgement on *what* to buy, but after that you are faced with the second issue of what to *do* with it.

Unless you are traveling with a support truck, odds are you aren't going to have room on the motorcycle for much in the way of souvenirs. That isn't automatically a reason not to get any, but you do have to plan ahead (at least a little). Most cities will have a shipping agency available to get your priceless native artifact back home (for a fee). Some of the bigger ones (like DHL or UPS) will even box the item for you before shipping.

If you are going to ship your treasure home right away, try to find a shipper first, and whether they will package for you. Also work out how taxes and export duties will be addressed (if at all, but there should be something). Make sure you have a safe address to ship to back home as well, since you might not be at your address to collect packages for a while.

Of course, all that assumes you know in advance that you'll be buying something that doesn't fit on the bike. More likely you'll be walking through a market and just *see something*, and then haggle to buy it. Even though it's after the fact, you can still take your time to work out shipping (assuming you aren't just passing through the town), and get it on the way safely.

Obviously - blankets ship better than crystal, so just keep that in mind.

Sleeping Bags, Pads, etc

Unless you are going to spend every night in a hotel, or some location which has a nice bed all set up for you, you are going to need to carry a "bed" with you. For most campers (and I am primarily thinking about campers during this section), this bed will consist of a pad or cot, and a sleeping bag or blanket. There will be exceptions (there always are), but most people will use some combination of these two things.

First off, I think having a good sleeping pad and bag is the most important part of camping. These two items account for a very large portion of my gear budget, even though I know many people rate getting a good tent higher. I can't disagree that a bad tent would be a disaster, but I also think you can get a pretty good tent without spending that much money. Most of us are traveling with a motor, which means weight means a little less to us than, say, a backpacker. I know, you can still overpack a motorcycle, but if you are going to carry some extra weight, having it be a higher quality, sturdier house make more sense than extra pants.

So, if you are willing to have a heavier tent, you can spend the money you save on a better sleeping bag and pad. Being comfortable while sleeping makes all the difference in the quality of your sleep, which affects how well you can enjoy the day. I hadn't known how *uncomfortable* I had been at night until I almost froze one night in Denali. This prompted a quick trip to Anchorage and REI to get a bag rated for lower temps, and an insulated pad. The next morning, I woke up feeling better than I had for weeks. I'd been cold at night and not sleeping well, but hadn't even noticed until I fixed the problem.

So, pads. I know there are going to be some people who use cots, and love them, and I'm fine with that - though I prefer and recommend a pad instead. Primarily, this is due to the insulation effect of a pad to provide warmth. You do lose some heat to the pad/ground when you are sleeping with one, but you will lose more heat with a cot due to the convective cooling of the air under the cot never warming up as the pad or ground would. So, while it might be more comfortable, it's not as warm. As for whether it's really more comfortable is up to personal preference, but I am pretty sure you can find a pad to fit your needs. I prefer inflating pads (open cell) to the firm ones which roll up (closed cell). If you have mixed feelings about blowing up a pad when you camp, EXPed makes one with a built in pump. Pads come in different widths and lengths, so you can get one that fits you and your sleeping bag (which I will talk about more when I talk about bags), and some have temperate ratings just like sleeping bags. Most, though, will simply be insulated or not-insulated. Insulated pads are bulkier, heavier, and more expensive, but I think they are worth it. While I know many travelers have visions of warm beaches, or at least wonder why anyone would want to be somewhere cold, even for motorcyclists who are determined to spend every day somewhere warm and sunny, bad weather happens. While being too hot at night can be uncomfortable, being too cold is life threatening.

So, along with your pad you are going to want a sleeping bag. Some overlanders use a blanket instead, which is a little more flexible than a bag, but I still prefer bags for other reasons. When you are looking at sleeping bags, the temp ratings are the minimum where the bag will keep you *alive* overnight. That is a much different thing than keeping *comfortable*, so even though you get 15f bag, don't expect to be comfortable at 20f without any additional materials. I prefer to travel with a 15f bag, since it's comfortable (with some help) down to 30f or so. When it starts getting much colder than that I start looking for indoor sleeping arrangements (and planning out how to ride somewhere warmer).

The material used as fill for the bag is a matter of a lot of online debate. I still use down, since I am comfortable with my ability to keep the bag dry while traveling. For most non-backpackers, it's actually easy to protect the bags from getting wet with a little bit of care and attention. Generally, you will have to be more careful about it in the tent, rather than while it's packed on the bike. Down is still considered to the best thing for insulation, and is able to handle multiple compressions without losing any loft (which is important for keeping you warm). Having said how great down is, synthetic insulations are also pretty amazing, and will still keep you warm. They are also less expensive (or can be anyway), and much more forgiving of humidity (which will kill a down back in short order). I think it's far more important to get a bag with the temperature rating that fits your budget, than worrying about what it's stuffed with.

In general, I prefer sleeping bags with full length sleeping pad holders. Part of this is because I sleep a lot in hammock tents, and it's important to not roll off the pad during the night. I can also be a restless sleeper when on the ground, so having the pad and bag locked together keeps me from rolling on to the ground during the night.

I mentioned early "other things" I do to when it's cold at night and I am trying to be warmer in the bag. The first, simplest thing is to bring some clothes (usually what I'm planning to wear in the morning) into the bag with me. The clothes fill some of the space and provide small pockets of trapped air, which results in the inside of the bag being warmer. And, yes, that means I am not wearing clothes while I am sleeping. Clothing can be constrictive while you sleep, which can affect the quality of your sleep. When it's cold, I will still keep on thermal base layers, and I'm not suggesting you sleep in the buff, but try to have loose fitting things on when it's time for bed.

If you are looking for something a little better than wadded up clothes, you can get a silk liner for your sleeping bag. These are actually just long soil sacks with a slit up one side to make them easier to get into. It's hard for me to explain *how*, but let me just be honest and say silk is very, very warm. It's also thin and lightweight, which makes it easier to carry than something like wool or fleece.

Since we're on the subject of beds, let me just touch on pillows. I like having a pillow, but they are big and bulky and hard to travel with. I have, at times (especially when I will be facing a wide range of overnight temperatures) bring a small fleece blanket along camping, and will fold it up to use as a pillow when I don't use it in the bag as insulation. When I don't have the blanket, I carry a small pillow case and stuff it with clothes for a pillow, or fold up my riding jacket (which isn't as comfortable as you might think). I know you can buy special travel pillows - some that pack small and inflate when you need them and some that are puffy all the time - but they aren't cheap and none of the ones I've seen seem to be worth spending the money, over the methods I listed above. Remember, you are supposed to be spending money on gas, and I'm betting you already have a pillow case somewhere you can bring along.

Tents

Once you have your sleeping bag and pad, you are going to want some sort of shelter to keep them in while you are camping. Tents come in all shapes and sizes, and what works for one person is uncomfortable for someone else, so I am going to give you some general guidelines.

First, size. Most tents are rated for "man," which is a vague reference to how many people might be able to sleep inside. Like temperature ratings on sleeping bags, this number doesn't always assume comfort, so putting three adults into a three man tent can be a bit crowded.

If you are planning to keep anything in your tent other than your sleeping bag, then you should add (at least) half a person to the tent space for each person sleeping in the tent. So, if there are two people planning to use the tent, then you should be looking at nothing smaller than three man model. If you are all alone, then you should be looking at "one and a half" tents (yes, there really are such things), or just getting a two man (since they are usually the same price).

Once you know the size of the tent you are shopping for, it's time to think about height. There isn't a standard grading system for tent heights, so the basic decision you have to make it whether you want to be able to stand up in it. For some campers, this is a recuirement to get dressed, but for most campers all that is really needed is the ability to sit up comfortably. This brings up one style of tent - the bivvy. These are, essentially, waterproof covers for your sleeping bag and pad. Fancier models have hoops or poles to lift up one end (for your head), but there isn't much else to them. They are popular with backpackers and bicyclists, since they pack very small and are very light, but they aren't the best choice for long-term travel. There will be days, perhaps several in a row, where you will be spending time in your tent because the weather is bad or you are waiting for something, so you will want to be comfortable while inside. This is where being able to sit up can be useful, since it allows you some freedom of movement, where a bivvy is no more than somewhere to sleep.

If you want to be able to stand up in your tent, be prepared to both spend a lot of money, and to have to deal with a lot of weight and bulk. Even tents that promise to "pack small," can only claim to do so compared to other tents of about the same size. I (briefly) traveled with one of those tents with the attached garage. It was a great tent when it was up, but when packed it accounted for almost half my total space and a quarter of my total weight. That was just too much, and the excess space was just too much for me. I know other traveler's who love theirs, so it's all a matter of what you are willing to deal with.

So, what tent to get? Most travelers overspend on their tents, which might make them feel better about sleeping in it under all kinds of situations but really isn't needed. And, as I

144

have mentioned before, if you need an expensive tent to feel ready to camp all over the world then get an expensive tent. But why are tents expensive? For years, tents construction has been driven by the need to pack smaller and be lighter. There are a lot of ways to save weight and bulk on a tent, but most of them also rob the tent of sturdiness - and if you are planning to live in a tent for months or years, you want a tent that can stand up to some abuse. To make a tent that is small, light, and *strong*, is expensive, and that cost is passed on to you (along with a premium for high end gear, usually). So, do you need a small, light, and strong tent? You should definitely get a strong one, since it will need to take some abuse over the time you use it. Perhaps the best tent I've ever used was made from heavy canvas - I mean that tent actually stayed up, and dry inside, when a tornado passed within a couple miles (I was not in it, at the time). But, that tent didn't roll up very small, and the poles didn't collapse into easy-to-move sections. So, depending on what you are planning to use as your transport, a canvas tent might not be the best option (though I note a lot of "serious" truck overlanders also use canvas). For motorcycle travel, the best "real" tent I've ever used was an off-the-shelf Walmart model. It wasn't light, and wasn't particularly small (perhaps two feet long, when packed), but it was made from heavy materials that resisted damage to an amazing degree - including a floor made from the heavy tarp material which saved my air mattress when neighbors in lesser tents (which cost 10x or more) woke up on the ground.

145

I used it for more than 10 years, with at least one 6-week trip a year as well as a bunch of shorter rides. I actually still have it, but don't usually travel with it anymore.

Which leads me to my next topic - specialty tents. When I was in Alaska I made an impulse buy of a Hennessy Hammock tent. I don't usually make impulse purchases, but I had the Very Large tent at the time, and was tired of carrying it around. The hammock was small, light, and I knew that hammocks could be very comfortable. So, I bought one, and it changed how I camped forever. As I have told people, everyone knows that hammocks are comfortable (assuming you aren't worried about falling out of them - but camping hammocks are pretty good about preventing that unless you manage to tip them all the way upside down - which also isn't all that easy), so it makes sense that they would be good for sleeping. And, just to be honest, when I am in bed or on the ground I *do* sleep on my side - and toss and turn - but in a hammock I sleep on my back all night. There is always an adjustment period, both on the first few nights in the hammock and the first few nights when I get home, but I've survived.

What happens when there aren't trees? Well, I set the hammock up on the ground for rain and bug protection, using it as a bivvy shelter. It's obviously not as comfortable as hanging, but it's no worse than being in a regular tent (with the space issues I've mentioned above). To be honest, I don't have to sleep on the ground as much as you probably think -

with some time and creativity you can find a lot of places to hang a hammock.

Another type of specialty tent I've seen a lot lately are roof tents - these mount to a rack on the top of your 4x4, and you just open them up. With most of them, you can leave your sleeping gear in, so once the tent is up you are set. I have to admit, they look pretty cool and it seems like it would make sense to have the tent outside the vehicle to save space. It also gets you higher, so (theoretically) would provide some protection against predators as well. In truth, I think any predator that really wanted to could still figure out how to get in there, but that isn't the biggest thing I don't like about these tents - they are expensive (always something I think about). You need the tent, which can cost a few hundred but more likely cost to $1,000, but you will probably *also* need a special rack to mount the tent to your roof. The rack can *double* the price of the tent, and for that kind of money I would rather sleep on the ground. There are cheaper models out there, but they tend to weigh much more. I know I have pointed out that weight isn't something to worry *too* much about, but the weight of a roof tent is on top of the vehicle, which can seriously alter its handling and center of balance, increasing the chances of an accident or roll-over.

It's not really a "tent," but many solo or traveling couples simply build a bed inside their truck. The designs range from a simple air mattress in the back with some bedding, to complicated shelf and storage systems, but it means everything is *inside*, which grants more security than any soft sided tent, and (depending on the design) means there isn't much in the way of set up or take down needed. Of course, it also means you don't have a lot of personal space, so if you are planning to travel with a partner make sure you get along.

Cooking Gear

I like to eat. I especially like to sample the food from other cultures. I also hate to do dishes. All these things lead me to wanting to eat at restaurants a lot, but I don't. Or, at least, I resist the urge as much as I can. I can't say I don't ever eat out when I am traveling, since food and eating are an important part of most cultures, and experiencing those cultures are part of the reason to be on the road.

So why not eat out all the time? For the same reason no one eats out all the time - it gets expensive in a hurry. Since I like to spend my money on traveling, I have to make my own meals frequently - just as I do at home. Since I don't just want to eat crackers, this means having some sort of a kitchen to prepare food in. While it's possible you haven't ever thought about it, kitchens usually have three components - food storage, equipment storage, and a cooking area. Your traveling kitchen will also need these areas to be functional so let's take them in order.

Food storage. When on a motorcycle I like to keep all my food in one bag (usually my tank bag, since it's large and easy to remove). Keeping it separated from everything else keeps the rest of my gear from smelling like food, which can be nice in areas where you have to worry about predators or scavengers poking around your camp. That isolation also means I can move the tank bag to a table in a campground or rest area and have all my food there for preparation, without having to dig through things on the motorcycle. A similar method can be used for 4x4 travelers, though they usually have to worry less about something breaking into their tent in the middle of the night (depending on where they are sleeping, and where they are keeping their food.) People traveling in trucks (and RVs) also have access to cold storage, something harder to manage with other means of travel. Being able to keep food cold allows for a larger variety of food (or at least less concern over how long something will last), but it isn't a *requirement* for most travel kitchens. There are a lot of foods which don't require being kept cold (since there are a lot of people living in the world without access to refrigeration), so don't think you have to rush out to buy a fridge for your truck if you don't have one. A cold drink at the end of a day is nice, though.

If you are backpacking, keeping your food isolated from the rest of your gear can be more of a challenge. Usually, backpackers are eating out more than other overlanders (I don't include people on through-hikes in this group, by the way), and camping less often (if at all). Since they are getting more support from the local community, their needs for a travel kitchen is less.

Where to keep your cooking gear is a separate question. Ideally, it will be with your food. I hope you are washing everything throughly when you are done cooking, but keeping all the smells together makes sense. It also means all the cooking gear is in one place, which makes *actually* cooking a lot easier. Depending on your available space, this might not be possible, but it's still something to think about.

For your kitchen equipment - and I will cover stoves later - you wont need as much as you might think. I recommend a pot and frying pan appropriate for the number of people you are traveling with (or a couple smaller ones), so there is enough of whatever you are cooking for everyone. Obviously, if you are traveling solo, then you don't need as large a pot as if you are traveling with four people, and be careful about "overbuying," getting too large of a cooking pot "just in case." Assuming you cook at home sometimes (you do cook at home sometimes?) you should have a pretty good idea for the size you need.

There are a bunch of companies that make cooking gear for travelers, again mostly for the backpacking crowd. This means they are small and light, and expensive. Sometimes they're also made out of alloys which are supposed to make them stronger and lighter than traditional materials such as stainless steel or aluminum. Approach such materials with caution. I am not going to say they are all bad, but some (titanium in particular, though it's not being used much for cooking gear anymore) is terrible at heat transfer - which is an important part of cooking.

Those companies also make different sizes and collections based on the number of people traveling together. I know there are a lot of overlanders who buy the "solo" kits before they hit the road, and travel with them for months or years without complaints. Most of those kits don't come with a frying pan, though, and I personally won't travel without one. While soup and rice are fine and keep you moving while you are on the road. There is something about being able to cook a burger or fry chicken, just to mix up the meals some after a while.

If you don't want to buy a special set (good for you) or you got a set and it doesn't have the frying pan I just recommended, you can raid your current kitchen supplies for the missing items. While you are at it, also grab a few common cooking utensils like a set of tongs, a knife, and a small spatula (one of those with the rubber ends usually works for me). If you are leaving home for a long time, also grab whatever dish soap you have left. No sense throwing it away.

The kitchen items you already have might be a little larger than one of the (more expensive) camping versions, but you *already own* them, so there's no need to buy another one to save a few ounces of weight. And, since they are the ones you already have, you know how they work and don't have to worry about what to do with them while you are on the road. Now, if you are leaving your partner or spouse at home while you are traveling, you should probably ask before you start taking things.

There was another lightweight motorcycle book I'd read which recommended not bringing a stove. Most of the meals suggested where made with cold ingredients, with eating out as a way to get other options. Campfires were also suggested for coffee or tea, or "warming beans." I don't know about everyone, but I like to be able to actually prepare meals while I am on the road just as I can while at home (to some extent, anyway). I am also not a fan of "warming beans" as a meal. So, I carry a stove. This also makes getting that first warm drink on a cold morning a matter of a couple minutes, rather than having to rebuild a cook fire.

Last time I looked there were about seven million different models of camping cook stoves on the market, so there are a lot of options to choose from. Apart from convenience factors, they only differ in two areas - how good their temperature control is and what fuel they use.

Fuel first. Assuming you have a gasoline engine, you should have a gasoline burning stove. This means you don't have to carry special fuel just to cook with, eating into your available cargo space. I know there are models of gel-burning stoves which promise no-fuss, no mess cooking and incredibly fast boil water times, but once you leave the country you bought that stove in, good luck finding the canisters of fuel. Also, you are going to have to carry those canisters (small pressurized containers) around until you need them. If you run out, there's no using the stove until you get more, while if you have a gas burning stove and run out of fuel for it, either you can steal from the vehicle or (if the vehicle is also empty), you have bigger problems.

Now, if you don't have a gasoline burning engine, you can still get stoves which burn your fuel of choice (unless you are pedaling or walking, in which case you should probably use a multi-fuel stove just to be safe). Since stoves come in three basic choices - gasoline (white gas, usually, which is closer to Kerosine than the stuff from the pump, but I've been using regular unleaded for years in my Coleman), gel, and multi-fuel, what sort of fuel you are already using can help you choose.

While I suggested *not* using gel stoves, the differences between multi-fuel and straight gas stoves might be less clear. It might seen like the multi-fuel stoves are a better choice since, you know, they can use anything. Also, since they are built for backpacking, they back nice and small, and those MSR bottles look cool strapped to things. Also, those bottle can be a reserve fuel supply, especially for a motorcyclist (since a liter of gas, which is the largest size those bottles come in, won't get a truck very far). The downsides of multi-fuel stoves are that they require assembly, which can be messy (as in, you spill fuel everywhere) and they are expensive (which is always a problem for me).

I do have a multi fuel stove, which I use as my backup, or when I am traveling with more space than I usually have on my motorcycle and can "afford" a second stove. My primary stove is a Coleman 533, which is still available online and from some retailers. Usually the stoves are listed as Coleman x33, where the number in the x spot represents different tank sizes. The stoves require no assembly before use, are simple to light and clean, and the parts are all still available from Coleman. Usually you can get one for less than $50.

The best thing about the Coleman, and why it's still my go-to stove, is its temperature control. It can boil water as quickly as you might want (burning through fuel in a hurry while it's at it), but it can also be turned down low enough to actually simmer foods or cook pancakes. My multi fuel stove, an MSR Simmerlite, which is an excellent stove in its own right, can't manage that range of temperatures - especially the lower temps needed for a lot of cooking.

You should also make sure that your pot and pan and other things work with your stove (aren't too unbalanced or too large for the cooking surface). If they are, rather than investing in a new stove or cook set, (which will be more money you could use for travel), look into a small stand which can hold the pot over the stove, rather than having it rest directly on top of it. You can usually find them in camping sections for people cooking over fires (who need something to hold their pots and pans over the flame), or you can make something with a bent up metal coat hanger and wire cutters. Just remember you have to pack whatever you get, so think about what you use.

Trip Prep

There are no secrets to success. It is the result of preparation, hard work, and learning from failure. - Colin Powell

Route Planning

Our goals can only be reached through a vehicle of a plan, in which we must fervently believe, and upon which we must vigorously act. There is no other route to success. - Pablo Picasso

Maps and Guidebooks

I love maps. I mean I *really* love them. Nothing makes me happier than spreading out a bunch of maps on a table or booth or floor and trying to work out where to go next. Or where I am now. I get lost a lot. I think being lost is a wonderful place to be.

My tank bag always has a map in it, slowing fading in the sun. I am lucky enough to live near a map store, where (for a while, anyway) everyone knew my name. I have drawers full of maps, and sorting which ones come with before I leave home is part of the fun. When there is somewhere giving away maps, I take one. Every time.

So, while you might say I'm biased, but it's not as bad as you might think. I *do* use a GPS. There are times I have be somewhere, or find an address, and then a GPS is incredibly useful. I don't want anyone thinking I live a GPS free life since I don't. But there are things I use a GPS for, and things I use maps for. Each is a tool, and should be used appropriately.

For example, route planning is simply easier on a paper map, where you can see more detail from further away. It's true that some computer programs (which can export GPS route) are starting to come close to what a paper map can represent, but there is a while yet before it's the same. Even longer before it's easier to pull out your computer on the side of the road to see where you are going. The largest fail is, as you zoom out to a large few on a computer or GPS screen, you lose detail on the map - smaller roads simply vanish. This means you can't see all the available routes, even if you know where you are going. If you are just exploring an area it's even less help.

Pre-planning is also much easier on a paper map, where you can see all the places you want to go. Don't be afraid to write on the map (assuming you bought them, I don't recommend it at libraries), since those notes might trigger a memory once you are on the road. As you mark spots and roads that interest you, a route may just appear - linking everything up for you.

While I know there will then be a temptation to build that route into your GPS, so you have a nice line to ride all the way - don't. You can put the various waypoints in, and those might be helpful if you need it or find yourself wandering far off course, but resist the urge to have your GPS handle your navigation.

When you are just riding the line on the screen, part of you disconnects from your environment. You don't really *have* to pay attention to where you are going, since you have a voice or prompt that will tell you when it's time to turn. If you rely on your paper map for navigation, you have to look around, to *pay attention* to where you are going and what you are passing, since you are dependent on your observations and mind for directions.

Now, I'm not saying never use GPS. I still use one when I am in an urban environment or other situations when I need all my attention on traffic and just being safe. I still miss turns, but if I miss a turn, or can't make it safely, the GPS will adjust my route for me - I don't have to look at the map, traffic, and road signs. But when I am just riding through a country, or in smaller towns where traffic isn't as much of a concern, then the GPS is off and I am using my eyeballs.

All that *sounds* great of course - but how to you *find* places to stop and see in the first place? While you might have a few places you already want to visit, there are probably hidden gems and locations you would regret missing when you found out about them later. For those places, there are guidebooks. Probably the most famous is the Lonely Planet series. It seems like there are Lonely Planet books for everywhere, and they have good recommendations on where to stay, what to see, and how to eat. They also do a good job of highlighting one of the weaknesses of guidebooks. Lonely Planet guides are written primarily for backpackers - travelers who do not have their own transportation. So, things to see and places to go assume you need local transport. Places to stay are often focused on locations near bus or train terminals. These aren't usually the best for overlander travelers, who need secure parking for their vehicle and grocery stores for their food.

Most guidebooks have a bias of some sort or other, so if possible try to read multiple publishers for the places you want to go. Take notes (or scans) of relevant parts, and add things you learn from online forums, written by other travelers about their experiences. Some keep really good notes on where they stayed and what they got while there, so don't be afraid to contact them and ask for suggestions (by the way, I remember places I stayed but not always how I got there. I like being lost but it does interfere with my helping others).

If you find a guidebook you really like, buy the digital version (unless you already did) so you can easily bring it along with on your trip (without filling your luggage with books). I usually end up with a dozen or so eBooks, which I reference while on the road for ideas when I am looking for something new to do.

Lastly, no matter how much you plan before you on get the road, don't be afraid to cancel or change plans while once you have started traveling. Things will come up, new ideas will be presented, you'll hear about something awesome which wasn't in any of the guidebooks and you have to go and see. Or, somewhere you were going to stop for the afternoon you decide to spend a few days instead. These moments and times are some of the best parts of overland travel, so don't worry if your dates and times end up being off. Go slow, take your time, enjoy the places you see - rather than trying to see a lot of places.

Cheap vs Expensive Countries

For long term travel, the budget will loom over just about everything. This includes your route planning. In the early stages, it won't affect things in the same way it will after you've been on the road for a while, but one of the important concepts you either need to plan for early on, or work in after you're on the road, is the difference between expensive and cheap countries.

Now, while expensive countries are usually the more developed ones, it's not a hard a fast rule. Relative currency exchanges between your home and where you are is a large factor, but there's no getting around the fact that the cost of living in some places is just less than in other places. I remember a book, "The Four Hour Work Week," which I'd picked up because who doesn't want to only work four hours a week? One of the huge, main points he makes in that is to work online where the cost of living is high, and actually live where it's low. So the four hours of work you do pays for everything where you are living.

As a system, that's broken down a little with people living in those countries always willing to work for less. But that doesn't change the point, and it applies just as equally to travelers.

When you are planning your route, odds are you will plan to pass through countries with different rates of exchange and standards of living, and your converted, home, currency will buy different levels of luxury. Depending on how tight your budget is, this could mean rushing through expensive countries to loiter in less expensive ones.

Again, need to clarify. Inexpensive is not the same as developing. For example, parts of Southeast Asia are very inexpensive for Americans to travel in. Some of this has to due with currency, other things with policies to encourage tourist travel. The result is a dollar goes a long way.

In other countries the dollar doesn't go as far. Also, the cost of other things (fuel, for example) is higher. This can result in budget-wrecking expenses while traveling, unless planned for. It's also why so many travelers tend to end up in the same places in the same countries over and over again - if you are looking to stretch your money as far as it will go you need to be in a favorable country for the stretching.

When to Travel Where

I have some friends on their second trip around the world on a motorcycle. They say their main goal when deciding where to head next is to always be riding in spring. With the world getting more connected all the time, this is increasingly becoming possible. Of course, I also regularly see their pictures online - covered in snow and ice and cold. I guess spring is still an unstable time of year. Personally, I'm aiming for always traveling in summer, but given my occasional brushes with tornados this might not be the best idea.

When you are route planning, you should try to learn the weather patterns where you want to visit, and when things might just be impassable. In Central America they have an impressive, but extremely regular, rainy season. Even during the rainy season, travel is possible, just know that between hours x and y, you need to find shelter. Early on in Guatemala, I was riding through HueHue and suddenly all the motorcycles got off the road - under awnings, into parking garages, it was the oddest thing. A few minutes later it started to rain. I mean, really, *really* rain. Pot holes large enough to swallow my motorcycle filled with water, and I decided they had the right idea and got off the road. Over the next few days I learned it rained from a little after 1 until a little after 2, every day. If I was out at 1, I found somewhere to sit and wait while the rains came. Then, one day, it stopped happening. It took a few more days before everyone started to trust the weather had changed, but it had. No more rain in the afternoons.

This leads to my next point. By the time the rains stopped, all the roads in the direction I wanted to go were flooded or washed out. The Pan American Highway, to the south of where I was and on the other side of the mountains, was closed. I was stuck, but it was a nice place to be stuck in.

Learning all this before you leave may be difficult or impossible (the rainy season is well known, but the conditions of the roads following the rainy season changes from year to year), but it still something you should think about before you choose when you are going to be places along your route.

And, since I was talking about budget earlier, I am going to bring it up here again. If there is a tourist economy where you are traveling (and there are likely to be a lot of places with a tourist economy where you are traveling, since those places are usually pretty cool to see), there will be a large difference in prices depending on whether you are there during their peak times, as opposed to their "off-season." Learning when places like Machu Piccho or The Grand Canyon experience peak crowds, and then planning to arrive as far from those times as you can (While still in weather you are willing to travel in, this time is sometimes called "shoulder season"), will not only save you money but drastically change how you experience those locations. The most shocking difference I've ever experienced was when I went to Yellowstone in late spring. I had friends who were going to be working there for part of the summer, and I went to visit them (and meet a woman I was then going to travel for a while with). The park was empty. Yellowstone Lake was just breaking up, the cracks and creaks of the ice was so loud. Bear jams - that chronic issue inside the park - only had a few cars and didn't really jam up anything. The hiking trails were deserted and pristine. You could, at times, feel completely alone.

If you've ever been to Yellowstone during the summer, then you know about the crowds, the traffic, the noise, and the bear jams. If you haven't, then despite all I've just written you should still go whenever you can. Even during peak season, it's an amazing, unique place and worth the time. Of course, if you can get there early or late in the year, it's even better. If you're really bold, go in the winter.

So, to recap - try to learn the weather and road conditions where you are hoping to travel in advance, and try to plan your route to take advantage of favorable conditions. Also, work out peak and off-peak tourist times, and travel in off-peak times as much as possible.

Now, the catch. Odds are the off-peak times are going to be the bad weather times. So, many long term overlanders are constantly skirting the edges. Bad weather either just cleared or is on the way, and the tourist season is just wrapping up or looming on the horizon.

And this is why my friends get to post pictures of snow and ice.

Solo Or Group Travel

Again - in the interest of full disclosure - I have spent almost all my time - all but a very small percentage - traveling solo. For years, the running joke in my life was the best way for me to end a relationship with a woman was to take a trip with her. While I really, really want to make it work, I admit it's a struggle.

This personal failing is linked to what I think is the strongest advantage for the solo traveler. There are no compromises when you are solely responsible for your time and route. Of course, this means that you are solely to blame when things go wrong, but that blame is easier to face when it's only your trip or time at risk, without the added pressure of another's dreams or expectations.

Solo motorcycle travel brings the additional advantage of heightening the apparent (well, actual, lets be honest.) vulnerability of the traveler. This vulnerability makes it easier to connection with locals who may be less eager to chat with or even approach a group. Also, being solo, it's easier to look for and accept these connections. It's the only sure defense against the loneliness of the road.

There are disadvantages to being alone on the road - beyond the loneliness I just mentioned. First, and most practical, is financial. As a solo traveler you have to bear all the costs involved. There is no sharing of rooms or ferries. Over time, these costs add up considerably, so accepting you will have to pay for everything is an important consideration for people going it alone.

The other major disadvantage to solo travel, and the reason many people choose to travel in groups or with a partner, is the amount of risk. If you are alone, as I mentioned, you are more vulnerable. While this makes you more approachable, this doesn't take away that you really *are* more vulnerable when you are alone. This means you have to much more aware of your surroundings and of the levels of risk you expose yourself and your vehicle to while you are on the road. If something goes wrong, there isn't anyone to go for help. If you are in a sketchy or dangerous situation, no one has your back.

A much less vital reason, but still a real one (and a reason tour groups are so popular) is as a solo traveler you also have to do all the planning and paperwork for your trip. Some people really like this stuff, but others would much rather get on the road and start seeing things.

So, what about traveling in a group then?

Traveling in a group means shared costs and experiences. You have someone to talk with about your experiences as you have them, rather than waiting until you find someone you share a language with, and who wants to hear about your trip. You also will always have someone to take your picture when you're somewhere cool.

The major downside of group travel (for me, anyway) is their lack of flexibility. When you are traveling in a group, the group has to move and act together. It's less able to spend an extra day somewhere or bypass one planned thing for another opportunity. Depending on the group, it might not even be possible to start a conversation to get the group moving in a different direction - even if most would agree with the idea - for fear of upsetting one person or causing an argument.

Groups are also much less approachable than solo travelers, especially when the group is speaking something other than the local language. The language and the group form two barriers to locals, and most won't try to overcome them. I personally don't like giving up the approachability, even though it come with the added risk of being alone.

Perhaps the type of group travel which hits all these weaknesses is a planned tour group. These (usually) do an excellent job of isolating the travelers from the locals (except for tourist interactions), while keeping to a set plan, route, and schedule. Some do allow route flexibility, but as a whole tour groups don't want their charges wandering around aimlessly.

Of course, where tour groups excel is the planning and prep. If you want to arrive, or to just be able to travel without worrying about the paperwork, medical needs, even repairs and maintenance, then look at traveling with an organized tour. They aren't all the same, so take some time to do research before you fork over money.

Now, I admitted in the beginning that I was a solo traveler, and struggled with groups. So, I know that much of what I said can be read as negative towards groups. I don't mean for you to rule out group travel or tours and a means to see the world. As I have also said in other places in this book - it matters more to me *that* you are traveling, than *how* you are traveling. I am not immune to knowing some people - for any of the reasons I listed above - who don't want to travel alone. I even know many people who take tours and enjoy them immensely. Any of these methods are perfectly valid ways to travel. Saying one is always better than the others ignores there are a lot of different people in the world and on the road.

Paperwork

The sweetest joy, the wildest woe is love. What the world really needs is more love and less paperwork. - Pearl Bailey

Vehicle Stuff

It isn't necessary to imagine the world ending in fire or ice. There are two other possibilities: one is paperwork, and the other is nostalgia. - Frank Zappa

Insurance and Registration

Traveling with a vehicle adds freedom to your trip, but it also adds complexity which isn't always easy to deal with. Odds are, while you are still home, you have to pay monthly or annually for insurance and registration to be able to drive on the road (legally, anyway). You might be hoping, once you are safely out of the county, you can get away with skipping these and just take care of it again before coming back home (if you come back with the vehicle at all).

Sadly, it doesn't *quite* work that way.

Along with registration, yet get a license plate. In my state, that plate has a clear expiration date. I mean, you look at the plate and you can tell. So, if I am in another country and the police look at my plate, if it is expired, and if they are in the mood, give me grief over it. This means I have to keep my plate current, even while I am on the road. Your state may also require proof of insurance in order to renew the registration, so you will have to pay for insurance at home even while you are on the road, at least long enough to get your registration current. Assuming you can get your registration renewed, you will also have to get the paperwork (stickers, in my case) shipped to wherever you happen to be in the world. This means you will need a friend or family member with an address in the right state, who is willing to forward them to me when they arrive. Oh, and I need to take care of all these things with enough time and fore-planning to be able to get them in time.

Some states are stricter about their licensing and registration requirements. Virginia, for example, will suspend your driver's license if you don't have insurance. While this might not both you so much while you are in Africa, eventually you will come back home (even for a visit), and you will be facing fines to get your license back. Or, if you are driving around with a suspended license (because you didn't know), you could face arrest - which wouldn't be the best homecoming. So, find out the requirements needed to say legal at home before you leave. Some states (just to make you feel better), also allow you to report the vehicle as "not driven on public roads." While you *can* then keep it registered, you might be able to avoid the insurance and some of the other taxes and fees. There are a lot of different rules in all the different states (not to mention people reading this who aren't from the USA), so find out your local rules.

Back home isn't the only place you have to deal with insurance. Most other countries will require you to have some sort of insurance while you are traveling through them. Some, like the EU, require to you to obtain it before arriving. Others, like through Central America, you buy it at the borders. There are even some situations (like when Americans enter Canada) when their home insurance may work in the new country. *Most* of the time, you can obtain insurance when you enter a country for the first time, but there are some things you need to know about that insurance. It's almost always liability only (which means you are protected from paying for damages, but your own repairs aren't covered). Also, in some developing countries, it might not even be that effective. You will be responsible for everything in the event of an accident, even if you aren't technically at fault (since if you weren't there, the accident wouldn't have happened). You will still need to get that insurance at the border, since police and checkpoints will be checking to see if you have it as a potential means of harassment.

I don't mean for this to sound intimidating. In truth, when you are in countries where the insurance is meaningless, you really are extremely rich (generally), regardless of you budget. Most of the time, the costs of an accident aren't overwhelming, only inconvenient.

While you are planning your route (and seeing if you need to get visas or other paperwork before arriving at the border), you will need to also look into insurance, what you need and where to get it. There are websites like Borderhelper.com and HorizonsUnlimited.com which will provide current information on what you need to get through most borders in the world.

Carnets and Shipping

I have to start any conversation about Carnet de Passage talking about import duties. When you enter a country with anything of large monetary value (a vehicle will always qualify), you are responsible for *importing* it into that country. Most of the time, this is a temporary import, since we will bring it us when we leave (hopefully). Temporary import duties are usually less than permanent import duties, and usually handled at the border. Some countries don't charge anything, only making a note of what you bring in and checking to make sure you leave with it. Other countries charge you at the border (usually based on the age of the vehicle, but there are some who take the time to look up the actual cost). When you leave the country they are supposed to refund that money. Lastly, there are some countries which don't monitor vehicles coming and going as closely, instead working to catch illegal vehicles in other ways.

Just as a side note - don't pay cash for your import duties (when you have to pay them). Put it on a credit card. If you don't get your refund have the credit card company try and get it back for you, rather than fighting yourself. If you *do* use cash, you will struggle getting the refund as few borders have cash on hand (to give out to people leaving, anyway).

Now, if you leave the country without the vehicle, then the import duty you paid is lost (since, you know, the vehicle was imported). Countries do understand that things happen. There are ways to handle accidents or theft to get the import duty refunded without having the vehicle (usually just matter of getting an official police report), but in general that's how it works.

A Carnet is another way of handling that temporary import duty. You obtain the Carnet (fully, a Carnet de Passage en Douane, or CPD) from an issuing organization (depending on where you live). A few years ago US citizens had to ask a Canadian or German service for one, but there is now a service here who will take care of it (www.atacarnet.com). Once you have the carnet, you carry it like a passport, getting your vehicle stamped into and out of each country you visit.

There are two ways to pay for the carnet. The first is a straight-up cash dump. You let the carnet agency know where you are going, and how much your vehicle is worth, and they work out the worst-case import duty you would be facing (since you would only have to pay it once), tack on an administrative fee, and send you the bill. At the time I write this, the worst import duties are four times the value of the vehicle (so, the cost of your vehicle times four - yes really that much). This fee is one of the reasons so many overlanders are in old, cheap machines rather than shiny new ones. If you come home *with* your vehicle, though, and have completed the carnet correctly, that cost is refunded (minus the fee, of course).

Now, if you have a $50,000 vehicle and don't have the $150,000 (plus fees) lying around, you can also take out a bond or insurance for your carnet (the issuer will have preference, and you probably have to go through them to obtain it). These are much, *much* less expensive, though you still can't just leave your vehicle somewhere (well, you can, but only under certain specific situations) and you still have the carnet to fill out correctly at borders.

Carnets aren't required everywhere. In fact you can ride around North and South America forever without one, even though some countries websites will claim they're needed. Before the bonds and insurance options, this made for travel in the Americas much simpler than other places in the world, since it saved the huge expense of the carnet. Now, with the bonds and insurances, carnets are less of a burden, and at the same time fewer countries are requiring them. You can certainly have and use a carnet even at borders you don't need one, and some travelers do just to avoid dealing with temporary import duties (in exchange for more paperwork and paying for the Carnet). If you have an idea of where you want to travel, ask other overlanders if they had a Carnet and needed it at the border. Once you have an idea of what you'll need for your trip, you can decide on what you to get.

Medical

We can lick gravity, but sometimes the paperwork is overwhelming. - Wernher von Braun

Insurance

It's a good idea, but by no means required, to have some sort of medical insurance while you are traveling. It's true that healthcare in most of the world is inexpensive, and that maintaining insurance at home is a huge drain on the budget (at least for Americans). So long as you might be coming home for medical care, it's a really *really* good idea to have some sort of coverage in place.

There are, basically, three kinds of medical insurances you should consider before you start traveling. The first is extrication or evacuation insurance. This is usually very affordable, and gives you a single number to call in the event of emergency. Once you call that number, and get them you location and condition, a medical team arrives, picks you up, and takes you home (and to a medical facility of your choice). Now, you don't automatically have to know your condition, just call the number (or have someone call the number for you) and their team takes it from there. The team will arrange all air and ground transport, as well as providing whatever care you need while you're being moved. For a (usually small) additional fee they'll even bring back whatever's left of your motorcycle (I don't think they handle larger vehicles, but companies are different).

The cost varies depending on where you are traveling, and how long you have the insurance for. One very nice feature is, in general (policies vary a little), it kicks in after you are only 150-200 miles from home. Which means, if you live on the east coast of the United States and want to go riding in the Southwest, you can purchase this insurance and, if anything happens, you get shipped back home for medical care. You don't have to be in Africa to crash, after all.

Which leads us to a health insurance plan. In the USA people are responsible for buying some sort of health insurance, though even people from countries with universal health care there are things you have to do on a regular basis to maintain that care. I recommend a plan with a high deductible, followed by total coverage. If you ever *actually* need the plan, it's going to be for something dramatic. That usually means a lot of cost in America's medical environment. Set aside the deductible in an account where you can't spend it, and it can serve as a nest egg for after the trip (hoping you never need it).

Of course, you don't *need* either of those two insurances, and can instead simply pay for whatever medical care you need while on the road. I know that might sound scary, but in truth a lot of the world has healthcare at least comparable to what is available in the USA, and for less cost (I don't mean to start a political discussion here, just pointing out something which you (hopefully) will never need to gain first hand experience in). In places which truly have no medical care, your insurance won't help anyway - except for extrication insurance. Assuming you can call the number and know your

181

location it will work anywhere. Of course, if you do have an accident in a place with expensive medical care, paying for it could mean the end of your travels for a long time.

There is one other type of insurance to consider, though it's intended more for short-term travel and to developed countries. Traveler's Insurance is a rider on your existing health care policy (if your country has universal health care, you might need to ask about this option. Sometimes it's included, and sometimes there is a small fee). Traveler's Insurance works in two ways, depending on the policy and country you're in. Either it works like "normal" insurance, where the bill goes to them, or you pay whatever the costs are and the insurance reimburses you when you get home. Obviously, the first option would be better, so look into the policies and how it will work in the various countries you are planning to travel through. Don't be afraid to ask questions, either - both from your insurance and from other travelers who have needed medical care while on the road.

Shots, Medications

Before you leave home, you will need to take care of some basic medical stuff. Most of this will be immunizations, some of which are just recommended and some (yellow fever) are required to travel to some countries. If you are really lucky, your regular doctor can take care of these things for you, but more likely you will have to find and see a travel doctor specialist. I used google and called around until I found one that accepted my insurance.

The doctor will want to know where you are going, and will probably give you a large stack of paper to read about the various medical dangers you might face while you are on the road. But they will also make sure you have all your shots. This is something you will need to start working on 8 months to a year *before* you start, since some of the shots (hepatitis, for one) are a series which have to be given over several months. Some insurance plans cover these shots, some don't, and some will cover a few of the shots and not the others. Check before your first appointment to avoid any shocks. If you live in the USA and near a border, think about crossing to get the shots in a foreign clinic. Even if you have to pay out of pocket, odds are it will cost less.

Which is another point to think about out. It is *possible* to get these shots and the other things, *after* you've left, on the road somewhere. I know travelers who have done just that. I am not going to say one method is better than the other (they are probably the same), but remember what I'd just said - some of the medications are actually a series, and take months to complete. So, while you can *finish* the series on the road, you might want to start them before leaving.

183

So, what are the shot options? Well, there are a lot. You should have your MMR and tetanus current, and you *need* yellow fever. After that I would personally recommend the hep C vaccination, though it's not required (it's just really effective). After that, there are dozens of options, all over which your travel doctor will go over. Take as many or as few as you need to feel comfortable traveling.

Apart from the shots, you will also get some pills. If you are traveling somewhere with malaria (and you probably will be) then you will be given a choice anti-malarial pills. You should know there are a lot of medications for malaria, but two are the most common preventative medications out there, and most overlanders in malaria areas are going to be on one or the other (or nothing).

I took Doxycycline, which I had to start a week or so before reaching countries on the malaria list my doctor gave me, and continue for a month after I'd left. Some people report weird side effect from Dox, but I was fine. At least, I think I was fine. It was also a *lot* of pills, which I'd brought with me from home. Once I started taking them, it felt like I was counting down on my time, which I didn't like much. To make transporting them easier I combined all them into one bottle. It meant the seal was broken, but they were stored in my personal kit and I didn't worry about it (otherwise it was 4 bottles, which would have been a lot more annoying).

Malarone is much more expensive than Dox, but users report fewer side effects. You can also do a search on both and find some Malarone users claiming Dox doesn't work at all and you should just buy the expensive stuff. I took Dox without issues. Last time I looked, one Malarone tablet was the same cost as 10-20 Dox pills, so I know which one I'd pick for a long trip through malaria country.

You should also ask for some sort of anti-biotic. Depending on the doctor, they may or may not prescribe some. If they don't, don't stress over it too much. If you need it, odds are very good you will be able to get some while you are on the road.

Depending on how long you are on the road, you may also need to bring along extra of any regular prescription medications you are taking. These should be requested through your regular doctor - and again be careful of sudden, large orders or your insurance may not cover the cost. Try to start getting extra pills as far in advance as you can, building up a stock to use while you are on the road (save the newest ones for when you are traveling, take the older ones before you go). All your medications should be transported in their containers, with the name of the medication listed. Don't mix different looking medications in the same bottle (even if they are the same pill), and don't use "per day" containers. While no one may ever look, a curious or over-zealous border guard (or one who is bored and looking to get a little extra money on the side) might find your mixed-up pills and accuse you of smuggling. While you should, probably, eventually, be able to get out that situation, it would be better to avoid it in the first place.

In addition to your prescriptions, you should carry a few over the counter medications. Tylenol (or acetaminophen, it's the same thing) for fevers. Ibuprofen for aches and soreness at the end of the day (or minor trauma). GI medications - one for if you can't go, and need to (stool softener, of some sort), and something if you are going and can't stop (anti-diarrhea). You shouldn't need hundreds of these (I hope), as they should all be available in cities while you travel. Don't over-buy or over-pack, since they have expiration dates. It's better to throw away 10 pills you never took than 50.

185

Budgeting

I have too many credit cards. You know what happened? Someone stole one and I didn't notice. I noticed when I got that bill. Whoa! It was so much less! I'm letting him keep it. I'm saving money! - Rita Rudner

Where Does The Money Come From?

So, it's actually a rather looming question when talking about budgeting - where does the money to travel come from in the first place? I mean, it's easy to budget nothing, it's just hard to travel on it. Not impossible of course, just hard (or more of an adjustment to what most people are used to).

Most people, when they take a long trip, work off a saving account. This money usually comes from either some lucky windfall, or (more likely) years of savings and selling off belongings before the trip. I cover more about how this might work next, but one thing to keep in mind when traveling from a fixed starting amount - that amount and how long you get it to last will ultimately determine the length of your trip. You have so much to spend, and once it's spent you will have to stop. That isn't a bad thing. As I said before, this is how most people fund their trips. Save money, travel, stop, save money again.

The other method of funding your trip is to set up or have a *recurring* source of income. This can be stocks, money from rental properties, retirement funds - it really doesn't matter. But you have money (hopefully enough to cover your travel budget) coming in every month, or quarter, or some predictable interval. This means, so long as nothing interrupts that income stream, funding won't affect the length of your trip.

Obviously, the second method sounds better, but it takes longer to set up and isn't without risk. Rental income depends on the property being rented, stocks aren't perfectly stable, and here in the USA we have quite a few stories about retirement funds being cashed out or cancelled, leaving people who expected that money with nothing.

Still, if you can set up some sort of recurring income to support your travel then by all means do so.

A third option - well, something you can do in addition to one of the other things - is to earn some money while you are on the road. This depends very much on your skills, what you want to do so you earn money, and your willingness to take time from your trip looking for work. Personally, I am terrible at this process and get distracted by being on the trip rather than worrying about how I am going to pay for the next day. There are also questions about being able to legal work in a country, trading goods or time for money locally (as opposed to working online). This sort of thing usually requires a different sort of visa than the tourist ones which most overlanders get. Worker visa are usually harder to obtain, and cost more to get in the first place. Not having the correct visa doesn't stop people from working while on the road, and (obviously) if you can work online it's not an issue.

Pre-Trip

Oh, the budget. I know a lot of people aren't fan of budgets, but it's something that has to be covered as part of a long trip. For most travelers, while on the road money won't be coming in - so what ever the funds are, that's all there will be. Of course, being able to earn enough on the road while traveling to keep traveling forever is a nice goal, but most overlanders are working from a savings account.

So, how to get money into that account?

Well, first you are going to have to take a long, hard look at where you are spending your money now. Cable bills, car payments, cell phone bills, all those streaming services - you are going to have look through those and figure out how to get rid of them. Yes, I said get rid of them. Not only are they money you could be saving, they will be a drain on your budget once you are on the road. Of course, you can get rid of some of those things right before you leave, but remember that you are supposed to be *saving*, so seriously think about the things you can do without.

For example, I had cable TV. It was about $150 a month, for the cable access and wireless internet at my house. For that money, I was watching about one hour of TV a week. Sure, there was the occasional evening or something I would flip randomly through channels, but I've always been more of a book reader. I was also lucky that my city usually had

189

something free every night I could attend. The one show I *was* watching (Mythbusters, if you were wondering) I could buy online and download at the library. My cell phone had unlimited data, so I could use that for internet access. I didn't need cable anymore.

When I cancelled it, I set up a new bank account just for the trip (okay, I already had done this - but you understand what I mean), and changed the direct deposit from my employer so the cable bill went into that trip account. This account didn't have a debit card, and it wasn't linked to my other accounts (so if I wanted money from it, I had to actually go to the bank). This meant the money wasn't easy to casually dip into and pay back "later." Money I saved by reducing bills was diverted into that account to found the trip, rather than being available to spend.

Now, I do have friends, and we did go out on a semi-regular basis for dinners and lunches. I didn't want to cut those, but eating out a few times a month gets expensive, so I would start inviting them over to my house. For the meals I would practice my camp cooking (using limited cooking supplies and ingredients, and single burners on the stove for each item) to produce a variety of small dishes for everyone to try (tapas, they are called these days). The dishes didn't always turn out…but I have understanding friends and I like to think they enjoyed this exposure to my trip. And I did still go out occasionally, being careful on my spending didn't mean I wanted to turn into a hermit.

How much you will be able to save will depend on your bills, and your ability to cut down on your spending. Obviously, you can't just stop paying your mortgage (until you're on the road, I guess, but selling might be a better choice) or making car payments (until your car is paid off, but yo don't have to buy a new one right away) - but as you start to think about long term travel resist the urge to replace or upgrade whenever you are done paying for something. This goes for things like your car, but also smaller items like cell phones. Most carriers now offer plans which don't include a phone subsidy, and these are less than the normal contract-with-a-phone plans. Letting the contract end also allows you to have your current cell phone unlocked, which makes it easier to use in other countries.

Any budget, especially a strict one, can be a challenge to develop and stick with, but you *can* absolutely reduce your monthly spending if you are willing. Focus on what the saving will bring you, and make sure those funds are set aside where you can't easily access them before you leave.

Post-Trip

Many overlanders want to be on the road forever. Even ones that start out just planning that one big trip for their life end up wanting more. If it's an addiction, I suppose there are worse ones.

But for most overlanders, trips come to an end. You spend a year or six or ten on the road, and then come home (or settle into a new home), and have to figure out how to do that thing other people call "normal life." Don't panic, breathe deeply, you got this.

First, you are going to have to do something with your travel equipment. If you still had a home to come back to, and ended your trip there, this is less an issue. You can just park, unpack, and it's all set. If you are ending your trip somewhere away from home, then you are going to have to do something with the stuff. If you know you are going to be finishing your trip in a different country than you started, make sure they will let you leave without all the stuff you arrived with (this is especially true if you arrive with a vehicle, since you will be responsible for import duties otherwise. I talk about this is another section). While just about every country will want some sort of explanation where the vehicle went, some allow the vehicle to be sold to other travelers, so long as it's still leaving. Some country's import duties are low enough that

192

losing the money isn't too bad, and can even be factored into the cost of the sale.

So who's buying, if you're selling? Well, I mentioned back at the start of this book one method of overland travel is to buy a vehicle and equipment from another overlander who finished their trip and don't want to ship everything home. There are internet forums for this sort of thing, such as Expedition Portal (more for trucks, but has everything) and the HUBB (more for motorcycles, but has everything) on Horizons Unlimited. Once you have the sale, you may or may not have to get some paperwork taken care of (the more documents you can throw at a border, the better, but if you can get the vehicle registration moved transferred into their name).

Depending on how much you have to sell (and your lifestyle), this will earn you anything the import duty and a flight home, to enough to live on for a while.

If you don't want to sell, or are thinking you won't want to while still planning your budget, you will have to budget for shipping at the end of your trip. Just like any other shipping you do during your trip, it's best to plan and book as far ahead as possible, even though the pressure of a shipping date can cause stress when it begins to approach. Of course, if you bring your equipment home, then you will have all the stuff for your next trip. Or if you end up homeless for a while you still have somewhere to sleep.

Since most of us leave jobs behind to travel, once the savings account is empty it's time to start working again. The fear of not being able to find work after the trip is one of the things people worry about before leaving, so taking some time to think about what you want to do when you get back is worthwhile.

Of course, you might have no idea what you want to be when you get back, other than something different. That's okay too. Don't let uncertainly for what comes "next" keep you from getting on the road in the first place.

Seriously, don't worry too much about it. While that might *seem* flippant (and I suppose it is, a little), if you are committed to taking the time to travel, you are going to have to accept the consequences of that choice. But, when you get back and are looking for work, don't *hide* the fact that you quit everything to travel. Highlight it. Talk about it. While you were on the road you faced and overcame problems and challenges daily. You became goal focused, learned to create and maintain a budget, gained self-confidence and interpersonal skills. Maybe you even picked up a couple other languages. One thing every job-advisor recommends it making your resume stand out from the crowd, and a long term overland trip is one really good way to manage that.

If you need to maintain skills or certifications on the road, see if you can manage it online. If you want to pick up new skills or certifications, see if you can get *those* online. Be careful of some online schools and training, since they aren't all the same. Especially if you are looking to change careers, take time and find out what recruiters want you to have, then work on getting those. It might seem obvious, but few job hunters work backwards in this way.

Being on the road for a while, and then coming back to a consumer society, you might feel a little overwhelmed. When you get a job and have money coming in again, you might also be tempted to start buying things. Try to resist this urge - you've proved to yourself that you don't need much to live on. While I am not going to tell anyone to live uncomfortably, remember that if you want to travel again you will be faced with selling all that stuff again. Instead, go back to saving. Few people, after one long trip, are done. Most overlanders can't wait to get back on the road (I know I can't). Put a map on the wall, draw some lines on it. Start dreaming.

Doing Good on the Road

I believe that every human mind feels pleasure in doing good to another. - Thomas Jefferson

Charities and Fundraising

Having a cause might be the reason you start traveling in the first place. Whether it's a family member who is struggling, or something you are just passionate about, raising money for a charity while on the road is increasingly common.

I am going to be honest. I don't work with charities while traveling. I travel for my own, personal, and perhaps selfish reasons - it makes me feel good. I enjoy seeing things and meeting people, and I don't generally want the extra responsibility of representing a charity, or trying to raise funds while I am on the road. I have, and will again, work with charities in specific situations, but will never hang *my* travel on them.

But, if you want to, and it's getting you on the road, then definitely do it. I just want you to know this is something I've talked over with other travelers who successfully used trips to raise money for causes they believe in. Since most of this book is my first hand experience. I want to be honest when it isn't.

So, there are a couple ways to go about raising funds. The first, and simplest, is to use your trip to gain attention for the charity. Then you put a donate button on your website, which allows visitor to give directly. A lot of charities have scrips on the website somewhere you can just copy and paste onto your blog to get it working. Facebook pages also have the option to add a button, and that button can also take the visitor to your charity's donation page.

If you want a little more control, or better record keeping, you can set up the donation link so it gives the money to you. Then you forward it to the charity on whatever schedule you decide on. As someone who would donate, I'd rather you used a direct link, so I knew that the money I was donating was being passed on. I have heard of people who set up donations for a charity, and keep part of the proceeds for themselves. Don't be too shocked, since this is basically what United Way and many other, large charities do to pay for their buildings and staff. So, it's not automatically wrong.

Another way to go about it is to contact the charity directly and see if they want to sponsor or support the trip in exchange for you providing some services or media events while on the road. If you can garner enough attention for your trip, appearing in some locations to talk about the charity might be a good way for them to raise funds at those events.

Either way you are going to have to generate interest and attention about your trip. Before you leave, but when you are well along on your prep (so people know you are serious), get on some internet forums and start talking about where you are going and why. Your signature on those forums should have a link to your website, and a direct link for funding your charity. Every post you make on the forums will have both those links, so people will see them (so long as you are posting

- so make sure that you are). Also contact your local news services, and some print or digital magazines that create articles about local events and businesses. Tell them about your trip, and what charity you are raising money for, and see if they would like to do so a story.

Another way to raise money is crowdfunding. While this doesn't *directly* support a charity, you can use some or all of the funds raised for the charity of your choice. Just be honest on your crowdfunding page. I haven't ever used a website like Kickstarter to fund travel (or anything else), but I've seen other people trying it with mixed results. If you aren't familiar with the process, crowdfunding asks people to donate an amount of money to your cause (whether it's travel or a new gadget or to help launch a new app - there are a lot of choices if you want to support something), usually in exchange for an item or gift in the future. What is given improves with the amount donated, from a thanks online to an all inclusive hiking trip (which I saw for a tent kickstarter). What you offer will depend on your resources, and the nature of your trip. Obviously, since you probably aren't building something, you will have to be creative with the material rewards (I know a couple authors who have funded books, so those books are among the things sponsors can receive).

Different crowdfunding sites handle the money differently. Kickstarter, for example, only awards money if a project is fully funded. Indiegogo has options where projects get the money even if their fundraising goals aren't met - which might be useful for general fund raising but a real problem if you've promised supporters something you needed the money to buy (which is why Kickstarter has that feature in place).

If you do use crowdfunding, make sure you are honest about how you plan to spend the money. There is a closed-supporter-email group created, and those people will want both the things they were promised in exchange for the money, and to know you are doing what you said you were going to do. Projects *have* simply fallen apart, either because the money wasn't enough to meet expenses or because of shady business practices, so try not to have that happen to you (or your next project won't do as well).

Volunteering

Doing volunteer work while traveling is a more direct way to benefit charities than raising funds. I am not going to say that raising funds is bad or unnecessary - I'm willing to say most charities would rather have your money (okay, they'd rather have both) - but providing *your own time* always makes a stronger impression than donating money. Our culture just views time and money differently.

So, you want to do volunteer work? That's good. If you are already working with a large charity organization to raise funds, they might have volunteer opportunities for you on the road. You might even get some place (very basic) to stay out of it, and some meals, but don't expect this. It would be a bonus. Remember you are there to *volunteer* - not get free stuff.

If you aren't working with a charity, or you are but want to do even more, there are services that work with overlanders and help them find vetted organizations they can volunteer with. Going through a service is usually safer than trying to find something on your own, since (hopefully) the service has done the work and found out if the organization is legitimate and worth volunteering for.

Of course, that assumes the *service* is legit. The way the internet works these days, it is surprisingly simple to set up something online with the goal of misleading people. That said, it's worth taking the time to find people in need to help, and helping them along your way. It will greatly enrich your trip, provide you with deeper connections with locals (which will have such a positive effect on your trip I can't even explain it), and raise awareness of those in need to everyone following you online.

While I did say to be careful, I would recommend the site The Muskoka Foundation. They've been around for a while, and are all over the Internet with their "do good as you go" movement. They have had a lot of positive reviews, and I know some overlanders who have gone through them and had good things to say.

Organized volunteering services aren't the only way to provide support to the communities you will be traveling through while on the road. Many of them, especially in developing areas, rely on neighbors to help with projects. If you pay attention, you might find these opportunities for yourself. As always, keep your wits about you and think about what you are being asked to do. Be careful about handing over money or transporting items, and if something ever feels sketchy or wrong, then don't do it - but try not to let fear rule how to treat people. It's not always clear what people intend, so it's best to be safe than sorry. Just don't play it too safe or you'll never leave home!

On the road

The best way to get to know the place you are traveling in is to walk around... - Laura Marano

Maintaining budget

A budget tells us what we can't afford, but it doesn't keep us from buying it. - William Feather

Keeping Track

Great! You are on the road. You followed some of my earlier advice and have an account set up, and you've transferred a week's worth on money into it. Now, it's day 4 of week one and - the account is empty. Where did the money go?

While I am not going to be quoting Mike Tyson much, he does have a perfect one for this moment - "Everyone has a plan until they get punched in the mouth." Your budget, carefully set up while at home, with however much travel experience you had before leaving, now will have to hold up for months or years on the road. Depending on that budget, situations like the one above can be annoying to terrifying.

Rule one - Don't Panic (also, quoting Douglas Adams is much more satisfying).

It's a good idea, especially in the beginning of a trip, to carefully monitor how much you are spending, and what you are spending it on. You will find there are things you need (or think you need) that you buy during those first few weeks, while at the same time you're packing other things up and mailing them home (or to an address somewhere for storage until you work out what to do with them.) It happens to almost everyone, don't worry about it. But those expenses, both buying the new equipment and shipping things home, wouldn't have been on the budget. *Actually living* on the road, as well, will have hidden costs that you never thought of (or forgot when I mentioned them), until you are on the road and watching the money drain away.

So, keep track. Since I like writing things down, I will go over that method first. I strongly recommend getting a small book and keeping a journal. Not just of what you spend, but also places you stop, people you meet, things you see - even how you're feeling and how the vehicle is running (you can also record maintenance and such here, unless you are tracking it separately. I like to have it all together). Set aside a section for expenses, and when you buy something write it down. Write it down right away - no holding onto a receipt and doing it later - then make it a habit to review your spending daily. I like to look it over in the morning, so I have a sense of where my finances are at the start of the day, but it doesn't matter when you do the review, so long as it gets done.

If you want to use something a little more modern (or you came from a life where you needed spreadsheets, and letting them go is harder than you'd thought), then you can track your expenses electronically. While this is a little more work, since you have to enter the data in your computer or phone or whatever, you can monitor how much you are spending, and what you are spending it on, much more accurately. I have a friend who knew, for example, how much money she'd spent on bottled water while traveling through South America. I could probably work it out, given time, but since she had it all on a spreadsheet the data was only a few clicks away.

Spreadsheets can also work out your currency conversions for you. Since you will be spending in local currency, doing the mental math every day can be a chore. Worse, if you don't know what the conversions are, you can end up spending more than you'd planned. Since you should be learning the exchange rate anyway, you can enter it into the relevant part of the spreadsheet as a conversion formula and it will work out the conversion for you (also, if you convert money at different rates - say at a border then later from an ATM or gray market, you can account for the different rates in the spreadsheet).

Obviously, you can combine both these into a single method - entering everything in a notebook during the day and updating a spreadsheet later - but here is the most import thing to remember. It doesn't matter *how* you keep track of expenses. What matters is that you update how much you are spending *often* and *regularly*. Set aside time, every day in the beginning, to go over what you spent and what you spent it on. *Pay attention* to it. Not so much that you stress and let it ruin your trip, but enough that you don't get surprised down the road.

During the Trip

Before I started traveling I did my budget monthly, if I was thinking long-term, or biweekly from paycheck to paycheck. Cover the bills, some for fun, a little set aside. Once I was on the road and meeting other overlanders I learned about something called Dollars Per Day.

Now, whenI first heard it I didn't really know what to say. I didn't have a daily budget, in fact those early trips didn't have a budget at all. I certainly didn't know what I was spending per day. But it seemed like most of the overlanders I was hanging out with *knew* this number (not all of them, thank goodness), and I didn't have a clue.

In truth, they didn't have a daily budget either. I'll explain.

When people ask me about long trips, there are two things they wonder about (whether or not they ask). Where did you find the time, and where did you get the money? I've talked about some of that already. Remember how overlanders are traveling varies so their budgets, both in time and money, also vary. If you meet someone on the road and want to travel together for a while, what the relative budgets are becomes important. Since no one wants to talk about how much money is in the bank (or at least rarely), instead they use a handy budget conversion tool - dollars per day.

I don't think anyone is really using a daily budget (which means someone is out there doing it, who I haven't met yet). I went with a weekly budget, since that was how often I arrived somewhere I could get cash. I usually stopped for a bit in those places and rested, did laundry, and serviced the bike if needed. I would take some time and go over how much I'd spent, and look at my overall budget since leaving home. While I didn't always take as good of notes as I would have liked, I learned there were three things I need to work into my budget while traveling. I started calling these things "the unavoidables"

The first I call Fuel, though it really refers to everything to do with your transport. For a vehicle this means fuel (of course), but also oil changes, tires, registration, *everything* to do with it. This also includes moving it from one continent to another. Shipping will be a major expense, so you want to plan well in advance and spread the cost over as much time traveling in the continent as you can. (Since if it costs $1000 to ship, that cost per day spread over the time spent before shipping will be a lot different if you spend weeks versus three years)

Food is the second unavoidable. While Fuel is for the bike, Food is for you. So, *food*, as well as health care, medicine, toothpaste, etc. I cook most of my own meals while on the road - for the same reason I cook most of my own meals at home. It's a lot less expensive.

The last unavoidable is Lodging. This covers places to stay. It could be lumped in with Food (since it pertains to you), but I think it should have its own category and budget.

Lodging can be either very cheap or very expensive, depending on where you are and what time of year you are there. Look for off-peak times and plan to arrive near the beginning or end of it (hoping for good weather). I camp a lot, and work to find free camping or places to stay as much as possible to keep this cost down.

When I plan a budget I work out the planned costs for things first (much like you plan for your mortgage before you put money aside for movies), and then do rest of my budgeting. For example, let's say I have a daily budget of $60 a day (this is about average for overland motorcycle travel, if you are moving fairly quickly. It drops as you slow down). For fuel, I budget $125 a week, food is $75, and Lodging $100. That's $300 a week for the unavoidables, which leave $120 for anything else I want to do along the way. Museums, tours, everything that isn't covered.

Now, that $60 a day is actually a pretty high for a budget. How much you spend per day really depends on two things - how fast you are going and what country you are in.

I know I keep bringing it up, but slowing down is simply the best way to save money. You have time to cook, and to find the food you need to cook. You can find inexpensive (or free) lodging because there is time to look for it. And of course, every day you spend walking around a town or sitting on a beach, is a day you aren't burning gasoline or adding wear and tear to the vehicle. Slow Down.

I mentioned before also, but will again, that there are some countries which are just more expensive than others. Prices of gas, food, camping, all vary from country to country, even ignoring the differences in exchange rates. Obviously your daily budget in inexpensive countries will be less than when in expensive countries. Focus on maintaining an average budget *over the length of the trip*, allowing yourself to spend more when in developed countries (which have more to spend money on on), then drag the daily average back down once you are somewhere less expensive. Be a little cautious about it, though. Don't go crazy in the hopes that you will make up the difference later. If you do go over budget (and you probably will), any cushion you've built up previously will be very useful.

Access to Funds

So you have these accounts with money in them, back in your home city or state. Now you are on the road in, well, wherever, and you need to get some of it. You can't just pop over to the bank and get your funds, so how do you get you money on the road?

The good news is that it's pretty easy. Yes, you *can* get traveler's checks (and some places even take them - but not many), but since credit cards have become accepted all over the world, so long as you have plastic you'll probably be okay.

I am not a fan of using a card to pay for everything. I find it harder to track my spending (I know, it should be easier since the card and computers keep track, I just fail to follow up on what I've spent when it's that passive of a process) and prefer to work off a pool of cash. Usually not a lot of cash, no more than a week's budget at a time. Cash is always welcome everywhere, especially little stands and markets that have the best stuff at the best prices.

I should mention, just as a basic security measure, not to carry all your cash, or all your cards, with you. Find somewhere on your motorcycle or vehicle (or in a boot) to keep most of it stashed, and use extreme caution when taking it out. It's best to only do that when you are in in the privacy of your room or somewhere similar. Keep a day's worth of your budget (or "walking around money"), along with a card if you are using one, with your driver's license, in your wallet. I don't carry a dedicated "mugger's wallet" anymore, since if I am being marked by a potential thief they are likely to know what wallet I am using for my purchases or to hold my ID. I just make sure your wallet only has limited resources, so losing it doesn't hurt (too much).

So, if you are going to use a card, use one that will have access to only *some* of your travel funds (like just your budget for the month, as an example). I used a PayPal card (which also gave cash back - bonus!), which was accepted everywhere I tried to use it. While PayPal was linked to my bank online, it was linked to a secondary account which didn't have all my savings. This meant I had to transfer funds into PayPal (after transferring them into the correct account) for there to be money on the card, but if the card was stolen only the funds PayPal had access to were at risk. PayPal doesn't officially have the same protections against fraud that a normal credit card has, though when I've had unknown charges on the account they've always refunded me the money.

One other thing I liked about the PayPal card was its lack of international card fees. Some cards (like another one I was carrying. I'd planned to us it, since it was linked directly to the bank account - until I started to get fees) charge a per-transaction fee while you are outside your home country. It doesn't matter if the issuing bank is also in that country - all that matters is that *you* aren't home anymore. These charges are usually "only" a couple of dollars (think of an ATM fee), but it quickly adds up if you are using the card to make purchases. This is something you need to find out about before leaving - to make sure the card you are using *doesn't* include these fees. It will be buried somewhere in the terms, but a quick internet search or call to customer service (which might not be that quick, I suppose) will also answer the question.

So, about actually *getting* cash money while on the road. There are basically three places to get cash - ATMs, Banks, and exchanges.

Looking at the last one first - exchanges - these require you have some currency to exchange for whatever the locals use. Many overlanders carry a pool of US Dollars for this reason. Dollars are acceptable all over the world, though both the official and unofficial exchange rates vary considerably (even in the same country). Knowing what the online rates are before you go looking to exchange one for another is a good idea, but it shouldn't keep you from bartering to get the best rate you can - or even guarantee that you will be able to get as good as the online rate is. Black market exchanges usually have better rates than official exchanges (official ones usually located near borders or in banks), though they always have a bit of risk associated with their use. I actually don't know of any overlander who was paying attention being arrested or harassed for using black market exchanges, but that doesn't mean it hasn't happened so use them at your own risk. You might also hear of "gray" market exchanges which are functionally the same as black market but they operate with the tacit approval of local government.

Which, in a way, brings us back to Traveler's Checks. Long, long ago (like, 25 years or more) these were what you used to travel internationally. They were pre-printed "checks" with your name on them. Banks, and many businesses, accepted them as cash (with change given in the local currency).

But that was 25 years ago.

Nowadays, you are better off asking a bank for a cash advance on a card than presenting them with a check, Traveler's or otherwise. Few businesses accept them anymore either, so the simple truth is that you are better off carrying a card. If you are worried about things being stolen, then have a back-up card stashed somewhere, rather than hoping to find someone who will accept a traveler's check while on the road.

Since I just mentioned banks, we'll cover those next. Banks all over the world will exchange currency, though the rates are usually terrible. You should be able to just walk in, present funds for exchange, and walk out again. Banks have an advantage of being easy to find and safe to use - though you might only get a fraction (and a small fraction) of the money you would have gotten on the black or gray market. I've never used a bank to exchange currency.

Very near to the bank, though, as well as all over the place in the world, are ATM machines. At this point in your life I'm guessing you know how they work. They usually get better rates of exchange than banks (though not usually as good as black market), and some will allow to you withdraw money in both the local currency and USD - which can be a nice feature. There are basically two networks around the world which ATMs use - Star and Pulse. If you look on the back of your card, one or the other (or both) of those should be listed. Both is best, obviously, since then you can use just one card everywhere (another advantage to PayPal). If you are in a country with only one network, and you don't have a card which works on that network, then you are pretty much out of luck for ATMs - or you will be paying even larger fees, depending on how the machines are set up. Or, you can use other money changing means.

While there are a lot of ATMs around (and ATMs were my primary means of dealing with funds), I limited the *number* of transactions by taking out money in chunks. This did mean I was occasionally cash-heavy, but it also meant I didn't have to pay as many fees. Fees add up in a hurry, and cash is accepted everywhere, so taking out a week's worth of budget meant I could just look and see how my spending was going for that week, and I only had to make four withdrawals a month (later it was down to three on average, since my spending dropped to the point my weekly budget was far in excess of my spending).

Unexpected Expenses

It is almost a mantra of overland travel. Things Go Wrong. Much of the time, it leads to unexpected adventures, amazing experiences, and new friends - but not all the time. Even the times it becomes a positive experience, odds are pretty good there a period of stress and anger (and wondering what you were thinking with this whole "travel" idea) and might be some large, unplanned for expense.

All that careful budgeting, too.

So, you have to face a sudden expense while on the road. Something seriously broke, either on you or on the vehicle, and you have to fix it. Depending on your resources, and how serious the situation is, it could even be trip ending.

That's okay.

First, take a deep breath.

We all face unplanned expenses in our lives - both at home and on the road. They are as much of a burden as we allow them to be. First, work out what needs to be done. If *you* or a traveling partner is injured, then get the medical care you need and don't worry about the budget. There are times to shave money, and times to just pay up.

If you are in an expensive country, this can be good and bad. Good, in that it's likely you will find whatever you need to get moving. Bad in that it will cost more. Once you have that cost worked out, or have paid it (either way you know what it is), look at your budget. If you are still on the road for a while, you can change your route to spend more time in less expensive areas to overcome some of the budget damage - otherwise look at removing or altering part your trip to take into account the unplanned spending.

In a developing country, you will have to find out if the help or medical care you need is even available. If it's something mechanically wrong, odds are pretty good you will find someone who can fix it. Local mechanics in small towns are amazing at putting together repairs. If not, see if you can get somewhere the repairs can be completed. Time tends to move differently in these situations, and you will be feeling more pressure to get things done than the people around you. Relax. Be willing to accept help but not demanding of it. Most people *will* want to help, if they can and you let them.

Once you have things on the way to sorted, look at your budget. You might find there simply isn't enough money left to keep traveling. First, remember slowing down is a great way to save, and if you are stopped anyway it's a good time to practice. But, if you really need more money to keep moving (or just want to extend your trip), there are ways to legally earn while on the road.

I say legally since, for the most part, overlanders travel on tourist visas in other countries. These are the easiest to get, but prohibit working *locally* while in the country. That means, for example, you can't pick up a quick job washing dishes for a few weeks while you wait for parts.

Except, of course, you *could*. It would be illegal and both you and the employer would be at risk. It would almost certainly be cash work, under the table and less than a local would be paid. Obviously, be careful with this.

A less obviously illegal method of earning is by making and selling trinkets or (if you have the skills) doing street performances. Again, be careful, especially in larger cities. These might need some sort of permit (which you will not be able to get with your tourist visa). Of course, if you are in your home country, these issues vanish and you can try to find odd jobs anywhere.

The most straightforward, and also legal, way to earn while on the road is to do something online. Depending on your job experience, there are many temporary freelance jobs available. If you have been traveling for a while, and have something meaningful to say about your experiences (or good pictures), it would also be worth reaching out to overland or travel magazines about your trip, pitching ideas for articles. Just so you know, some pay on acceptance, and others on publication (which can be some time later), and some in free copies (which is cool but doesn't help with the bills). Ask up front about this, so you aren't surprised.

One other online option, if you have a website and following, is to simply ask for donations. One of the first things I heard when I came home was a complaint from someone that I *didn't* have a donation link. They said they would have been more than happy to send me money, if I'd asked. I hadn't asked, so they hadn't sent any. The simple fact is, to travel, we need funds. Usually not a lot of funds, but still funds. If we want to travel, and keep traveling, we need to be willing to accept those funds from where ever they come.

Keeping Moving

If I'm traveling, I'll pack socks in my bag - really cute furry ones. - Nicki Minaj

Finding Fuel

Your vehicle has an engine. While that engine will need a fair number of things done to it on a regular basis, what it will need most often is fuel. Motorcycles in particular have a limited range, compared to larger vehicles, and less space to carry extra fuel and extend that range. The good news is that engines are common all over the world and all of them (well, most) will also need gasoline regularly. So, if there are people around, odds are pretty good there will be fuel somewhere as well.

That fuel, however, might not be the pure, high octane stuff you're used to getting. The 50 gallon drum on the side of the road might read "94 Octane" in black spray paint, but I have doubts. There have been a few times I've refilled in that situation, and it's important to treat it like any other barter. Work out the cost before they start pouring, so you know what you are spending. And, what they have is what they have - take it or leave it. It is nice to have a lower-compression engine that will run well on lower-octane fuel, but most motorcycles will be okay with questionable fuel (so long as it's the right kind - no diesel in a gas engine!) for a while. Some riders have reported using questionable fuel for months or years in modern, high-compression engines without problems, and others have had nothing *but* problems, so it's hard to say what your own experience will be.

Obviously, having a good fuel filter installed (and perhaps filtering the fuel as you fill your tank) is an excellent idea.

If you are faced with a situation where your on-board range isn't enough to get you to the next fuel, you will need to work out how to carry extra. Proper fuel cans, plastic or metal, are obviously best, but they can be expensive for something you are likely to use once and then get rid of (since carrying extra fuel just to carry extra fuel doesn't make sense - fuel is heavy). You could carry an extra, empty container around for when you *do* need it (I will, occasionally, when I'm in areas with limited fuel options. My motorcycle only has a range of 150-175 miles, and a gallon will add another 60), but most of the time I rely on my stock tank. While this does affect my routing choices, it's usually not a big deal and saves me the risk of carrying a container of valuable (in some areas) and flammable material strapped to my possessions.

If you have gotten somewhere you need more range than you have, and you *aren't* carrying an external fuel container, there are other options. One of the preferred ones is to use a soda bottle (or several) to carry the extra fuel. Plastic bottles are common all over the world, and are usually thrown away when people are done with them. They should be easy to find in whatever quantity you decide you need (of course, you can also just buy and drink some soda). Rinse them out well, and make sure they are thoroughly dry before adding gasoline to them (water is very bad in engines). Depending on where you are in the world, you may or may not be allowed to pump fuel directly into these bottles (some parts of the world, gasoline is sold in those bottles, but you aren't usually allowed to keep them). If so, you will need to fill your regular tank, then transfer the fuel to the bottles later (and then refill your tank). Once you are on the road, empty the bottles as soon as there is room in your main tank. This also applies to any external fuel container you happen to be using. As soon as you can, get that fuel into the main tank.

There are couple good reasons for this. First, it *needs* to be in the tank for it to reach the engine, so you're going to have to add it at some point. Second, once it's in the main tank you can stop worrying about leaks, or it breaking in a fall (for motorcyclists) and spilling gas everywhere. If you are using a disposable container, you can then dispose of it (unless you wait until it can go into a proper trash can). Lastly, once it's in your main tank, it's at less risk of being stolen while you are stopped somewhere (perhaps needing some privacy in the bushes). It's unlikely that other traffic will take the time to steal gas while you are parked, but if the road doesn't have a lot of fuel available (or it's locally expensive), who knows what people might do to get where they need to be. So, just pour it in and don't worry about it.

Finding Food and Water

Just like the vehicle needs fuel, you will need water and food, in that order, to keep moving. While water is far more important, finding food while you are on the road (especially food you can identify) can't be ignored or overlooked. The good news is that, where there are people, there is food and water. The quality and cleanliness of that food and water can vary considerably, and while the locals might be safe eating and drinking them (or aren't, as is often the case), a traveler just passing through might find his digestion "seriously disrupted" by partaking.

One thing about social customs - food and drink are frequently offered as a show of friendship and acceptance. So, if you are offered things you have no desire to risk eating or drinking, you should try to make a show of trying it. If the food and water are truly unsafe, odds are you won't be offered any. In fact, I've found I was offered the finest available food and drink. I've tried, when I could, to include my hosts in the meal, which occasionally was a far better meal than they would make for themselves on any but the most special of occasions (People in Ecuador were particularly stand-offish at meals, waiting for me to eat before coming near).

So, water first. While the internet will gladly give you numbers ranging all over the place, most health organizations report you need 2 liters of water a day. That water can come from other sources than *pure* water. Soda, coffee, teas, even soup, all will provide some hydration benefit (yes, I know that caffeine is bad for hydration), so you don't need to focus on drinking 2 liters of water on top of whatever beverages you have during the day. You will also need water for washing dishes, cooking, brushing your teeth, and other simple chores while camping. Washing up doesn't really need to use bottled water, unless the local water is particularly bad.

Bottled water is available in most towns and villages, and even more common in larger cities. If you are shopping in markets, confirm the bottle caps are sealed (to make sure they didn't just refill an empty bottle). If you are looking in shops, water might be in heat-sealed bags, like water balloons. These are less expensive and come in a variety of sizes. While I don't know where the water came from, using them never caused me any problems, other than needing somewhere to put the water immediately when I opened the bag. Unlike a bottle, there is no re-sealing the bag once you cut into it. I carry a hydration pack, so used these bags as refills. Water bottles I would tuck into my luggage and use as needed.

I do not travel with a water filter. While running out of water was the main reason I'd head to civilization (well, and someone else to cook, do laundry, see people, etc), the water filter products available when I started traveling were either very expensive, or needed regular replacement filters for long term use. Since I didn't want to carry filters along, and I wasn't sure I would be able to get replacements as needed, I just went with bottled water.

Since I started traveling, though, filtration has improved and there are now pump-style filters which last tens of thousands of gallons. They also claim to be cleanable and reusable, but with that lifespan I don't know if I'd need to worry about it. 10,000 gallons of water, at 2 liters a day, is 50 *years* travel for a solo rider - so it might be worth investing in (Sawyer, by the way, is the manufacturer I'm referring to - but by the time you read this there will undoubtedly be others). If you are going to bring a water filter, make sure it can remove both particulates and bacteria. If it doesn't, and you still want to use it, you will either have to add another filtering step, or boil the water before you can drink it.

Of course, you also need food. Food is everywhere there are people, though *what* food is sometimes be interesting. If you are cooking your own meals (which you likely will be, at least some of the time) then you will need ingredients. While in developed countries, there will be grocery stores and supermarkets, which will have things you know and recognize from home. In developing countries, while you might see the occasional small grocery store, markets are more common for food shopping (as well as most other goods, and some services). I was occasionally at a loss in some areas of local markets - having no idea what I was looking at - but I made it a point to try unknown things on occasion. Usually it didn't work out, at least the first time I tried something new, but I learned and found things I really enjoyed and was happy when I saw them in other markets (since only local goods are usually available. and just because something can grow doesn't mean anyone is growing it). Few things are labeled, either with names or prices, so having some idea what you are looking for is important. Remember that prices in markets are flexible - you will be expected to bargain. Depending on how good your language skills are, this can be all sorts of entertaining. Don't be afraid to try new things - or even familiar things which are subtly (or very) different than you are used to. I remember my first visit to a meat market in Baja. Carcasses were hanging from hooks, and the butcher was just chopping off the things people ordered (taking the carcass down for larger bits). Since I didn't have the right Spanish words to order, I just pointed at things and hoped for the best. I also made sure I cooked everything thoroughly before eating, and I never got sick (at least, from the food). Much of it was much better than anything I'd bought on a styrofoam tray wrapped in plastic back home.

Similar precautions should be followed with fruits and vegetables. Take the time to wash them (with clean water), before cooking if you are cooking them. I know there are some travelers who skip washing if the fruit has a peal (I've done this too), since the peal will, in theory, protect the actual fruit from contamination. I've never had a problem when I've tried this, but I've also always thought it was sketchy on the science. I guess you will have to use your discretion.

Staying Sane

For most of my life, I've traveled alone (other than a stuffed teddy bear, but he doesn't talk much. I have managed to find an awesome woman who plans to travel with me in the future). I'm also usually on a motorcycle, which means, when I'm riding, listening to engine hum and wind noise for hours. In towns there are people around, but I only occasionally run into other travelers, or even people who speak my native language.

This means I can go a little crazy, sometimes.

The truth is, there are now so many people traveling all over the world, you can almost always find someone to spend time with who shares a language and some experiences - but I've always thought prolonged travel with someone, especially someone who you share a language with in lands you don't speak the native language, isolates you.

Having someone to speak with, without struggling for words or drawing pictures or making crazy gestures, can make a difference in your mental health. So, it's important to make sure this happens, from time to time, even if you are spending most of your trip solo. How often it needs to happen will be up to you, but whenever you start getting depressed or road weary, it's time to go looking for other travelers.

Those travelers, depending on how their trip is going, may be in worse shape than you are, but even then it's someone to talk to who understands overlanding isn't always as much fun as it looks like on the posters (just be careful not to let other's bad experiences affect you or your trip). They may also have ideas on things to do, places to see, that you hadn't heard of and will reinvigorate your own travel. Or, they may not, but at least you will have another traveler to hang out with. There is something to the community of travelers which can be welcoming after being on your own, or even with friendly non-travelers for a while. It's hard to explain, so you will have to trust me when the time comes.

Even if you are traveling with people who speak your language, finding others to change the mix of personalities can relieve tensions or kill doldrums that might set in on a long trip. Meeting other overlanders might also mean traveling partners change when people start parting ways. Remember, always, that everyone is on their own trip - and relax and enjoy the journey.

Bad Weather

A lot of this section has to do with motorcycles, since they are exposed to the elements. I know weather is a factor for people who are wandering around with enclosed vehicles, but most of that is weather's effect on road conditions, and I'll cover those next.

Everyone likes riding when the temperature is just right, the sun is just so, and the road is smooth and runs on and on. But, if you are on the road long enough, the sun will go away, and the temperature will go too high or too low. All this will have to be dealt with as part of your trip, so you face the choice of waiting in place until things improve, turning around and going another way, or continuing on.

While it might sound like I am belittling the idea of stopping or turning back, I don't mean to. I've talked elsewhere about risk management. If the way forward isn't safe, then it's not safe and you should stop and wait (if you expect things will get better) or find another, more favorable route. While you were doing research, you might learn when the weather in certain areas should be favorable, and you can plan your route accordingly (chasing spring or chasing summer as it moves around the globe). The real problem is that many overlanders ride on the edges of peak seasons, when the weather is not always ideal. When the weather *is* ideal, the tourists start showing up and the prices start getting higher. Depending on the country, this might make travel very, very expensive. Or, it might not - your budget and the countries in question will decide for you.

Obviously, you can't stop every time the weather isn't pleasant and sunny. Well, you *can* but that will definitely slow your pace and restrict the places you can go. You should have, as part of your basic riding gear, things to keep you dry when it's raining. Most riding gear has some provision for this already, but not all of them, and you might need to pack special gear (if you need to replace your gear, then look for stuff that is waterproof). Also, as your gear ages, it might become *less* waterproof, which will mean adding a waterproof layer when needed. It seems my jacket fades first, and when it starts to leak I'll get an inexpensive waterproof to wear under or over it. I prefer to wear them over my jacket, since that keeps the jacket dry, but it does expose the waterproof layer to damage - not to mention needing one that is oversized enough to fit over everything. So, it's usually whatever is available locally when I decide I need one.

Staying dry is, by far, the most important part of staying warm while riding. Wetness robs body heat with frightening effectiveness, and cold is lethal when riding. Not only is hypothermia a serious medical condition, as your temperature starts to drop, so does your ability to make decisions and think clearly. So, when it's cool (as in, under 90 degrees - which is less than your body temperature before you start zipping around at 60mph) do whatever you need to stay dry.

Cold, without also being wet, is a separate issue. "Dress in layers" is something you've probably heard a few hundred times at this point in your life, but I am going to say it again. "Dress in layers." Okay, now that I've said that, what does it really mean to have layers, and why does it matter?

The important thing about layers is to trap air - little pockets in between the layers of fabric in your clothing - which help you hold heat. So, when you have layers, what you are doing is creating these little pockets of trapped air. This means it's better to have many thin layers on than a couple thick ones. Also, as I mentioned above, keeping your skin dry is important, so the layer close to your skin should be a wicking synthetic layer. Don't get me wrong, I like cotton, but when it's cold and you need to stay warm (and you're living on a motorcycle for months or years with a limited amount of stuff you can carry) then you need to bring what works, rather than what you want to work.

There is one other powerful aid for when it's cold - heated gear. This stuff (usually a jacket liner, but there are also gloves, pants, socks, enough to cover you from neck to toes) plugs into the motorcycle and runs off its electricity. This means you need your motorcycle to have enough extra electricity to power whatever heated gear you want - but most modern bikes can manage at least a jacket, and some can run more. Heated gear warms up like a heated blanket, which allows you to ride in much lower temperatures, comfortably, than you could without it, even with lots of layers.

One other thing to think about when riding in the cold is road conditions. While ice and snow might be around, there is something subtler and dangerous going on. Your tires. Most motorcycle tires are short-lived, soft rubber which wear out in a few thousand miles. Many overlanders use tires that last longer, both to save money and to reduce the number of times you have find replacements while on the road. Tires which last longer are usually a harder rubber, which seems obvious, but hard rubber doesn't warm up as quickly as soft rubber. Harder rubber also doesn't grip the road as well. Normally, as you ride, the tires warm and you don't notice a little less traction than you might have with a more aggressive tire. As a rule, overland riders don't push their machines that hard. But, when the road and air are colder, the tires won't warm up, and so won't grip as well. This means a simple, slow corner can cause your tires to slip, when they wouldn't have normally. So, especially when you just start riding in colder temperatures, be aware that you need to take the corners a little more carefully.

Along with cold, there is also hot. Extreme heat is actually a little harder to deal with than cold - adding layers and heated gear will help keep you warm but there are only so many layers you can loose when it's hot. I won't ride without armored gear and a helmet, so everything I do to keep cool has to keep me in my riding stuff. The synthetic clothing will help some, but the best thing is to regularly soak that layer close to your skin in water (if you can find it). Evaporation, especially while riding, will provide excellent cooling, at least until the fabric dries.

In both hot and cold temperatures, it's important to keep drinking water (or some form of hydration). It's easy to become dehydrated, in cold temps because your body won't want you adding cold liquids, and in hot weather because you are losing fluids quickly as your body tries to cool itself. As a general rule of thumb (and by no means scientific), if you don't have to use the bathroom every couple hours, you aren't drinking enough. Since most motorcycles have two hours of fuel, if you don't have to go when you stop, you aren't drinking enough and need to figure out how to drink more.

Beyond temperature extremes, there are also the joys of precipitation and wind. Ugh, a side wind is one of the worst things for a motorcyclist (and it can complicate other weather conditions). Motorcycles are light and tall. A strong, gusting side wind can actually push them out of their lane and off the road or into oncoming traffic (though it's good to know it doesn't happen often). Usually, it's just a push a foot or so, and easy to adjust for. Sustained winds mean you ride with the bike leaned to the side (like you're going around a corner), and results in a kinked neck for the rider. Head winds cause increased buffeting and fatigue, as well as greatly reduced fuel economy (which might be a problem in an area which has limited fuel availability). Tail winds, though can improve MPG, reduce fatigue, and cause this odd feeling of motionlessness if you are moving with the wind.

Rain, by itself, isn't bad to ride in. While wet roads can cause traction issues, tires are designed to deal with that sort of thing. When it rains for the first time in a while (usually a couple weeks, but it varies from road to road and place to place), a thin, slick layer can initially form. This is from rubber or oil left from other traffic, and if the rain continues it will wash away. If it rains regularly, or has been raining for a while, then this layer never has a chance to build up.

Snow is different. First, if it's snowing it's probably cold, so all those tips about staying dry come into play. Riding in snow is a unique experience, unlike any other riding condition. If your rear wheel spins too much, it will melt the snow, which might help you get to pavement or might just allow the wheel to keep spinning (on the newly formed ice). Other off-road rules about lowering your center of gravity by standing on the pegs, or keeping RPMs high, are much less effective in snow, since tires grip less as they spin more. Your best option is to take it slow and accept that you might have to paddle your feet from time to time, unless you are in an area that will let you use motorcycle tire chains, or spiked tires (which are used in ice racing). These will greatly improve your handling in snow and ice, but *reduce* it on other surfaces (metal doesn't grip concrete all that well).

Bad Roads

One of the things I had to learn, and learn quickly, was that I couldn't be sure about roads in developing countries. Think about all the times you are going around a corner - I'm willing to bet, of all the things you might worry about, that the road will simply end isn't on the list (usually).

What qualifies as a "road" can vary considerably from country to country, or even region to region. Even "paved" covers a lot of territory. Consider, in the lower 48 of the United States, "paved" means cement or blacktop. In Alaska, "paved" is bitumen, tar with gravel pressed into it scraped level. In Canada and Europe, it means anything along that spectrum, from cement to bitumen. In Baja, "paved" can mean that it was paved, at one point, but along the free highways (as opposed to the toll roads), repair and maintenance can be lacking. Since the weather is generally stable, a bit of gravel here and there doesn't bother any of the locals, so no one says anything.

Most maps will have a legend letting you know what the road surface is supposed to be. In most developed countries the road will be as described. In developing countries, especially well away from urban or tourist areas, what the surface will consist of can be anyone's guess. As an overlander, you have to accept whatever the road brings you, as well as what that road is made of. Just remember not to rush, and that it's better to be stuck than to be injured, especially in a remote area.

When driving or riding, try to keep your speed under control, regardless of the road surface. Especially in the desert or plains, where the road seems to stretch ahead forever and looks like smooth pavement. You would be surprised how quickly that smoothness disappears as your speed increases. Slight rises turn into ramps, and pot holes appear very quickly. In some countries, bumps are placed on these stretches just to keep speeds down (also going in and out of towns, and anywhere else they feel like putting one). Even hitting one at the posted speed limit can seriously damage a wheel, and if you are going too fast you won't have time to see it.

If the road isn't paved, you are probably faced with sand or gravel. Gravel, if it's well packed, is easy if you take your time. Speed will improve stability, but also increase your momentum if things start to go wrong (meaning injury or damage is more likely). Since I ride solo, I always err on the side of going too slow - which is also probably a good idea for people traveling in groups. In fact, it might be more important in groups, so there isn't any pressure on riders to exceed their ability so they don't "slow anyone down."

Sand is one of the more challenging surfaces to ride on (unlike mud or snow, which I'll get into later). You can reduce your tire pressures (which flattens out the tire on the ground, increasing the surface area and helping to keep the bike from sinking in), but to ride on sand successfully you need enough speed to stay on top, but not so much speed that you lose control (and the resulting crash causes injuries). Again, I tend to ride too slowly, since I'd rather have to get the bike unstuck than damage it or me. What that magic "just enough" speed is will vary on your bike, tires and tire pressure, how much stuff you're carrying, and even the type of sand.

Loose gravel and sandy surfaces share a special surface issue called corrugations. These are rhythmic waves, usually close together, caused by suspension bouncing up and down and compressing parts of the road more than others. When riding over them (or even driving over them, if they are bad enough) it's like being in a bad washing machine. The only way to smooth the ride is to increase speed - this will keep the tires from dipping into the lower parts of the corrugations. Whether or not you feel safe at the speed you need to keep the ride smooth is up to you and the road. Even if you think you'd kept the ride smooth, once you reach the end of the corrugations (or any time you stop for a break, if you happen to be on a long stretch of them) you need to check all the nuts, bolts, and fasteners for looseness. Yes, this can literally shake your motorcycle apart if it goes on long enough.

I mentioned earlier about mud and snow, and the way I did it may have sounded like these surfaces aren't as challenging as sand. Some of you, perhaps with experience in mud or snow, might have wondered what I was thinking.

Well, I was thinking there *isn't* any good way to ride in mud or snow. You are going to fall over. While there are special tires for those conditions, those tires are of limited use (or even dangerous) for all the other road surfaces an overland traveler might face. So, unless you plan on a lot of tire changes, you aren't going to be using those special tires. So, faced with real mud or deep snow, the only real choice is accepting the falls, waiting for conditions to change, or going another way. Which you choose will depend on your trip. So, what *did* I mean about mud and snow being less challenging than sand when I also said you have to accept falling? With sand, you *can* ride, though it takes some skill. Still, it is a skill you can pick up with time and practice. With mud and snow, while a skilled rider might do *better*, it's more in the hands of luck and physics. While that is difficult, it's too random for me to think of it as a challenge to my riding skills. Maybe to my sanity, though.

Borders and checkpoints

We always think of borders as something that separates two peoples but of course they unite them. It's something you have in common, literally. - Don Winslow

Some Simple Border Rules

International travel means crossing borders, and land borders are all kinds of different than flying. So, a few simple things to keep in mind when you are moving from one country to another.

First, every border is actually two borders. You are exiting one country, and entering another. If you get out of one, and have trouble getting into the other, it's not always possible to turn around and go back. You might get stuck in the middle until whatever you need to do gets taken care of.

Remember, you are trying to be a guest in their country. I am not going to say bribes and grifts aren't a problem at some borders (since they are), but for the most part, and most borders, they are just trying to do the right thing. So, before you start getting upset at delays or requests, ask yourself how you would feel about letting a screaming, angry stranger into your home (or country). Smile. Smile a lot. When delays happen, just keep smiling. It is hard to explain how effective a smile, with patience, can be.

You will need currency for the next country before you get to the border. There will be fees and charges you have to pay, so be prepared. Banks in towns near the border should be able to exchange money for you, and there are always black market exchanges if you need them. As always, find out the exchange rate so you have some idea of what you should be getting.

If you do exchange at the border, still have some sort of idea what the rates should be. Odds are you aren't getting a favorable rate at the border, since you (literally) have no where else to go.

Still, that's no reason to be ripped off, so pay attention. You can always exchange what you need to get through the border and get more money later.

I remember crossing borders in Central America, and the money changers would first ask how much I had to change, then type some numbers into a calculator and hold it up, showing what they planned to give me back. This worked well, since it meant we didn't have to deal with my terrible Spanish, but there were occasions the numbers they used didn't line up with current rates in any way. Just take the calculator (politely) and punch in something more favorable, just like any other bartering situation. You need money at the border, so you aren't in a great bargaining position, that doesn't mean you are powerless and shouldn't dicker some.

As you are given bits of paper (which happens a lot at borders), keep *all* of them. I had a folder I used for the country I was entering (and another for the country I was exiting), and I put all paperwork in as I went through customs and immigration. That folder was then presented when needed at checkpoints and when leaving the country for all the exit paperwork. The old stuff would then be filed away before I started entering the next country, and its paperwork would go back into another folder for "completed" countries. You never know what, exactly, you are going to need later, so just keep everything.

On helpers (as they are called in Central America - many other places call them Fixers). I used helpers and don't regret it. I know others who did and wish they hadn't, or felt ripped off, or who didn't use helpers and have the same complaints (or lack of them).

242

The choice to use helpers is personal, therefore, so it's hard to have a recommendation. I would say, unless you have an excellent command of Spanish and have spent time online working out all the things you need to know and locations at the border you have to visit, at least through Central America you should just use the helpers. From what I understand of Africa, similar rules apply - it's much easier to use a fixer than trying to figure it out, though you *can* figure it out if you really want to. Other places, it's up to you (If they are even available. I haven't ever seen one between the USA and Canada).

Paperwork

Borders are about paperwork. They love, *love,* their paperwork. You need to have all of yours in order to get through a border easily (or at all). You also need to keep it all in order while traveling inside the country. Not everywhere has internal security with checkpoints - but I find it's easier to keep everything together and straight, especially when I do have to produce it all from time to time (so long as nothing goes missing when you keep showing it).

As I mentioned previously, every border is really two - out of one country and into another. Also, you have to get two things through each border. You, and your vehicle. So, it becomes four crossings at each border.

While that might sound daunting, it's not worth staying home over. And, the border is there to monitor traffic and keep out some things - definitely not to stop tourists (and overlanders fall into that category) from coming in and spending money.

So, to get through border is pretty simple if you break it down into smaller chunks. To leave a country, you present your passport and visa (which should be in your passport). They will make sure you haven't overstayed, cancel the visa and stamp you out of the country, and you're out.

The vehicle (unless it's a bicycle) is a little more complicated. If you have a Carnet, it gets stamped out just at customs. If you don't have a Carnet, you have to complete whatever paperwork you were given when you entered, indicating you left with the vehicle.

This is important for getting any temporary import duty you paid refunded. You aren't likely to get cash, so make a note of the date and start checking to make sure the card you used (assuming you used a card when you entered, like I suggested) is refunded. How long refunds will take varies from country to country, so ask. Of course, not every country collects an import duty when you enter, instead looking to collect when you leave without your vehicle. If you did lose your vehicle while in the country (through theft or an accident) have whatever paperwork you were given ready for the border personnel.

So, once you have everything "stamped out" of the country you've been traveling through, you are in the no-mans land between one country and another. When both borders are at the same location, you just move meters down the road, park again, and start the entry process. This isn't the case at every border though, and you might have to travel a while to get to the new immigration and customs control. Also, immigrations and customs might not be at the same place. Crossing from Nicaragua to Costa Rica, customs for Costa Rica was a small building between the borders. If it wasn't for my border helper, I would have missed it (so that helper was worth it).

To get yourself into a country, you will need (at least) a passport. Depending on your home country and where you are entering you may also need a visa (which is official permission from the country to enter). Some countries you can get visas at the border, others you have to get it at an embassy before you arrive. Some countries want you to get the visa at their embassy in your home country - so checking the visa requirements for where you want to go is something you need to do early on in your planning. In addition to your visa and passport, some countries will want proof that you have vaccinations against diseases. When you visited the travel doctor for your shots, they should have given you a yellow form with what you got and when you got it listed. For countries looking at this information, they will be primarily worried about Yellow Fever, but to be honest I've never had anyone even check my form while I was traveling.

You may also need copies of your passport photo. How many (and if you need them at all) will depend on the border. There have been times when I was supposed to need extra and no one asked for them, and I've heard of border crossings where it didn't matter how many photos the traveler had, the staff wanted more (which they would provide for a fee, of course). Once you have all that paperwork taken care of, you are through and into the new country.

Just like you, getting the vehicle over the border is a matter of having the right documents. First, and most important, are the ownership papers. In the USA this is the title. I recommend making copies of it, and then getting at least one laminated. It's going to be passed around a lot. If you have a Carnet, this is also the time to pull that out. You will have to deal with getting the import duty taken care of (if needed, I talk about how different countries handle import duties elsewhere). You will probably also have to buy some sort of insurance, unless you arranged for it in advance (again, some countries require this be taken care of in advance). The worth of this insurance will vary depending on the country, but almost every country will require something.

You may also have to deal with some sort of fumigation cleaning. This can be just rolling through a ditch of water, to a complete and thorough inspection with fines and cleaning fees. Traveling through regions with drug issues (like Central America), may include an inspection from the local version of the DEA, with a bit of official paper saying it happened. You may also need to get copies of all this paperwork and bring it to other offices in other buildings. While a lot of it will seem like needless busy work, try to relax and keep smiling.

Depending on the border, you may be asked for fees or other payment during this process. Try to do some research before arriving to learn what things like the visas and temporary import duty will cost (as well as any other costs, like the fumigation), so you can have the money in the correct currency before arriving. Even if you do this research, plan for extra charges, just in case. Be alert for random fees or things costing far more than expected, but there might be smaller extra fees. Whether you just pay these to move on, or dig in your heels over the graft will be up to you. For the best information on border costs, check web forums such as Horizons Unlimited. As a resource for getting through a border, I haven't found any single location on the internet that has better up-to-date information.

Checkpoints

Once you are through a border, you might still have to deal with checkpoints or other controls while traveling through the country. Not everywhere has them, and they range from official checkpoints to improvised locations set up by local police or military. And, before you start thinking it's only something you will have to deal with in developing countries, the USA maintains several such checkpoints.

Most of the time you will be asked for your passport and the paperwork you were given for your vehicle. They will primarily be concerned with making sure you entered the country legally and have all the proper paperwork from the border. They may also want to look at the motorcycle or vehicle just to look at it.

Just like at borders, keep smiling and follow their directions as best you can. Depending on the situation, they may be far more interested in your vehicle than your paperwork. I get a lot of pictures of guys in uniform sitting on my motorcycle.

You might run into some checkpoints which are "sketchy." Keep your wits about you, and if you are on a motorcycle keep in mind you are more vulnerable than some other travelers. If there are areas which aren't under government control, it's worth avoiding them. A few years ago an American motorcyclist went missing, and later was found dead in an area which had been overrun with warlords. Among overlanders it was known to be unsafe with no military presence, but he went off with a false military convoy. This is one of the reasons it's so important to connect with overlanders while on the road and be aware of the situation in the country you are visiting.

Of course, even at legitimate checkpoints you might face some sort of fine. Away from checkpoints, you might be faced with something informally called "tourist fees." These are false charges or even completely made up laws which you will be found to have broken. Usually the officers will hold your driver's license and tell you they won't return it until you pay, or threaten you with jail time, or require you to wait a few days, then report to the police station to pay a (larger) fine and collect your license. You can't just ignore the chance of jail time, but if you have multiple licenses then losing one to the police station is an option.

Or, you can just pay the "fine" and move on with your trip. Most of the time they ask for $20 USD, and I usually carried a $10 in my wallet with plans to offer it when needed. It only came up once (and I had actually done something illegal at the time) and the officer took the ten without complaint.

I can't over emphasize the importance of maintaining a positive attitude during these interactions. Smile. If you feel like they are trying to shake you down for money, then smile, shake hands, and lose any command of the local language you might have picked up. Be willing to wait, smiling, patient, and pleasant. All these things might not be enough, and you might have to pay. While that hurts, and might offend your sense of right and wrong, sometimes it's the only option.

Being on the road means you have some risks different from staying home. But to keep traveling you have to manage those risks as best you can.

Staying connected

Friends show their love in times of trouble, not in happiness. - Euripides

Internet

As overland travelers, the internet is our friend and companion. It's also our lifeline - where we go for help and direction, and to find company when the road feels empty.

At home, you probably don't think about internet access much. You have cable or WiFi at home, the internet is on your smart phone, most stores and restaurants even have open WiFi for you to use while you are there. Being online is so easy that when you find yourself disconnected it can be a shock ("what do you mean I can't check the weather?"). So, where *can* you get internet connectivity while you are traveling? This section is not going to cover getting your phone connected to local cell service (which I covered elsewhere), and streaming internet I'll cover later (most phones can also connect to WiFi, so that's good).

The good news is, in most of the world, the Internet is as available, and important, as it is in your home country (where ever your home country is). I was particularly surprised in Mexico, where many public squares, even in small towns, had WiFi (although it wasn't always particularly fast). Many hotels, and just about every hostel (ones up in the mountains or deep in the forest excepted), also have WiFi for you to use while staying (or hanging out in the lobby "waiting for someone.")

If you want faster speeds, some parts of the world have dedicated Internet cafes. These are usually set up with computers, and charge by the hour. If you are traveling with your own computer, you can simply move the Ethernet cable from their computer to yours. If you *have* to use their computer, be very careful about the websites you visit and passwords you enter. Many cafe computers have malware which can capture your keystrokes as you enter them. This is why it's better to use your computer with their cable, rather than their computer (if you have a choice).

One thing which can be a shock are internet restrictions. I don't mean how Google.com becomes Google.ca when you get to Canada, but there might be places and sites on the internet you simply can't get to, either with a blocked page or 404 error). There are countries with internet filters and restrictions that might be surprising if you are used to a free and open internet. If you need them, there are IP filters which can mask your location and allow you to get around the internet restrictions. While I was aware of these internet restrictions at times, I found they didn't bother me and I was able to do the things I needed to while online. I didn't spend much time surfing the internet while traveling, since there was always something that seemed more interesting.

There were unexpected bonuses to international travel. While I am not a huge fan of American football, I'm from Wisconsin and have friends who always wanted to talk about the Green Bay Packers. It shouldn't be much of a surprise to learn there wasn't a lot of TV coverage outside the USA. When I'd cut cable before leaving, I'd looked at streaming packages for games, but they were extremely expensive (hundreds of dollars). Once in Mexico, the cost dropped to only about $30 (at the time). I didn't know this right away. It was mentioned while I was staying on a beach that had a nice bar. The bar owner was from the USA and needed his football, which was even broadcast in English, though the captions were in Spanish.

My point is, if you need the internet *and* are in a population center, you should be able to get online without much trouble. It might not be exactly the same experience you are used to, but that can be good or bad depending on your point of view.

Phone

I admit it - I am a little lost when I don't have my phone. I use it as an auxiliary brain, to take notes and pictures, monitor my budget, even do some journaling. I still use a paper journal to document long winded thoughts about things I see while traveling, but I really do love my phone. To borrow another's phrase "all my friends live in there."

So, when I leave the USA and my phone is no longer a phone, just a music player and camera, I notice it's missing. It also makes it harder to find friends once I arrive in a new city or town. I know, it wasn't that long ago no one had cell phones and we all managed. My first trips had me looking at check-in boards at campgrounds and using pay phones to check in. It *could* be done and, to a lesser extent, still can (pay phones are a lot harder to find). There are fewer check-in boards at campgrounds - the ones that do are in poor-cell areas (or they would have gone into a fire long ago). Pay phones have almost vanished, but if you really go looking you can probably find something.

Lets face it, the world has moved on. It's just more connected now.

So, if you want to be sure you can look things up or stay connected with family and friends, a working cell phone is simply the best way to do it. Naturally, it's easier than you think.

First, some background - there are two types of cellular phone technology - CDMA, and GSM. GSM phones work all over the world, and CDMA phones work in the USA. GSM phones *also* work in the USA, but CDMA technology is only here. Why it works this way gets a little odd and complicated, so I am not going to get into it. If the politics of technology advancement interests you, then it might be interesting.

If you don't know which phone you have, there are two easy ways to check. First, go online and do a little research. It shouldn't be that hard to find out, but if you don't want to do that there is an even easier way. Does your phone have a SIM card? If, yes, it's GSM (or at least, will work on a GSM network). If you didn't get a SIM card then you probably have a CDMA phone. There are an ever increasing number of models which work on both networks, so it might be worth double checking with an internet search.

So, you have a phone and you want to use it in another country. First, you need to get it unlocked. This allows you to put any company's SIM card in the phone and activate on that network. If you bought the phone as part of a contract, that contract has to be complete before you can have the phone unlocked. If you don't have a contract, make sure you aren't making phone payments (which is how many companies in the USA are doing "no contract" plans for new phones. The cost of the phone is spread over two years like a loan, with the balance due if you leave). In most cases, you have to clearly own the phone to have it unlocked.

If you followed my previous advice to get out of all contracts, then this shouldn't be a problem. Get the phone unlocked, and when you get to a country where you want your phone to work as a phone, get a SIM card (pre-paid ones are available all over), put it in the phone, activate, and you're all set. Yes, it really is that simple. There are also "world" SIM cards you can order online which work in a variety of countries (so you don't have to keep getting new SIM cards and activating them over and over). The plans are a little more expensive, but if you don't want to deal with getting set up with a new plan every time you cross a border, they are worth considering.

If you don't have a SIM card phone, or don't want to travel with a phone all the time and need one temporarily, then you can pick up complete, pre-paid phones inexpensively all over the world. These are usually "dumb" phones, without all the connectivity or features of a smart phone - but if you are just looking to make some calls it will work fine.

One thing to monitor with any pre-paid plan is that it's unlikely to have the number of minutes, texts, or data you are used to with the plan you had at home. That doesn't mean that it won't be enough, or that you can't buy more, but think about how long you are going to be in the country and what you are planning to use your phone for before settling on a plan. Sometimes it's better to buy a little more at a slight increase in fees, than have to buy another inexpensive package because you didn't have enough.

One thing I haven't mentioned are satellite (or Sat) phones. These don't work with a local cellular network, but by contacting satellites directly. Because of this, they really do work everywhere (or at least everywhere they can make contact with a satellite - which is far more coverage than you will find with any cellular network). At one time these phones were insanely expensive, and most mere mortals couldn't even consider them. Now they are only ridiculously expensive (Iridium, admittedly the gold standard for Sat phones, has a monthly plan of $70 for 20 minutes talk time), and I expect the costs will continue to come down over time.

Usually, you can rent a phone (these are special devices - you aren't going to find one in a store) along with paying for a plan. Think of these as voice-only devices. You might be able to send a text, but forget long emails, web browsing, or backing up pictures and video. Still, it's one thing that will work *everywhere*, so for many overlanders (especially ones planning to spend a lot of time remote and in dangerous terrain) the cost is worth it.

Shipping things home

I don't have a lot of personal space at home, so buying things to keep in my living room when I get home (so I can show it to people and explain where it came from) isn't high on my priority list. I did buy a few presents, and early on there were things I decided I didn't want along, and sent those off to wherever I needed them to go.

In the back of my Journal (you are all traveling with a journal, right?) I had pages set aside for addresses. Some I already had listed when I left home, others I added while on the road - people I met and wanted to stay in touch with. Post cards were easy, but if I found something nice that I wanted to send as a gift, it was just a matter of choosing who I wanted to send it to and finding somewhere to mail it from.

Sadly, as I mentioned, it's not always gifts you need to ship. Many overlanders, leaving on a long trip, find themselves overloaded after a week or two on the road and need to get rid of some stuff. Since the traveler in question probably spent a lot of money on that stuff, they won't want to just throw it away or abandon it on the side of the road. If there are other traveler's around, one of them might take something another is discarding, but you are probably going to have to ship it somewhere. I go into this with a lot more detail earlier in the book, so hopefully you remember.

Having an address you can send things to while you are on the road for storage might also work if you need a "home" while you are on the road. Occasional borders or checkpoints will want to know you have a "home" you can refer to and give the address of.

Also, when you have things you don't want, or buy something you want as a souvenir of the trip but not to carry on the rest of your trip, it gives you somewhere you can ship it.

Ship it how? Well, most major cities have pack-and-ship companies (like UPS or DHL retail locations), where you simply bring the item and they box it up and ship it for you. You will have to pay for the service, and the shipping, and for any export fees (if it's leaving the country). This last item might seem daunting, but you just have to declare the value of what you are shipping (which you know, since you bought it) and are then responsible for export duties and taxes. If you brought the items into the country, you can try to explain this and avoid the export duty (since you brought the items in with you, you can hardly be responsible for paying to export them - you would have to pay a lot more at borders!), but I can't guarantee it will work. Obviously, if you are going to send extra stuff you packed but no longer want to carry, shipping it home while you still in the same country has real advantages.

Getting things shipped to you

As I mention in my packing talks and elsewhere in this book, it's impractical to carry everything you might need in the way of spare parts, along with you on a motorcycle (or truck, for that matter). Since *anything* might break, you would need a complete second vehicle to make sure you had whatever was needed. This is actually a good reason for motorcycles traveling together to be on the same make and model of bike (not to steal parts, but to use one bike to test parts for failure so you know what needs replacing, and so you don't have to carry as many spares), but even then you aren't carrying replacement parts (unless you come to hate your traveling partner and leave them stranded somewhere), only parts you can use for testing.

So, you might have to get something shipped to you, either from home or an online dealer, to make repairs. Most of this section will deal with getting things shipped from home, though some will be relevant to both situations. Most online dealers (not all, by any means) are aware of what they need to do to legally ship parts internationally (which is why some won't). If you do need to order parts and have access to a local dealer or motorcycle shop, try to order it through them. It might be more expensive than if you order online, but the local business will know who to contact for shipping and what they actually need to do to *get* the parts. They have to, or they wouldn't be able to work as a business.

Assuming you have someone at home who knows what parts you need, and has access to a collection of parts (I left a nearly complete motorcycle with my mechanic), or an online dealer who you trust but doesn't ship internationally. You need an address for them to ship to. If you aren't sure, there are some UPS stores which allow you to pick up items shipped to them. Ask first, before anything is actually sent.

Any parts being shipped should have a used look, even if they aren't used, so before they are boxed they should get some dirt and grease smeared around. If this would be bad for the part in question, then don't (obviously), but if the package is opened for customs inspection you don't want it to be too shiny (since importing used parts for repair is less expensive than importing new parts). There should also be a note, or several notes, stating the parts are for a temporarily imported vehicle's repair, and not staying in the country. In a way, you imported these parts when you took care of the temporary import duty at customs, and will be leaving broken parts behind (of "no value"). Even with this, if the customs agents want to harass you they will. Just like at a border, try and stay calm and smile a lot. Offer to bring them the broken parts or to show them the inoperative vehicle (which they might have to travel to, but it's not working, right?). Again, working with a local business they can contact for information might help.

Another thing to consider is *which* shipping company to use. I mentioned UPS earlier, but that wasn't a recommendation. And, I suggest that if you have a favorite, go-to shipper, you let go of that prejudice while on the road. If you need parts shipped to you, find out who delivers to the local businesses (again, look for car or motorcycle repair shops to ask) and use them. If you are in a large urban area, it may or may not matter much, but I strongly recommend you *always* find out who the locals use for their shipping, and then make sure whoever is shipping to you uses the same company. Both UPS and DHL (the two major ones) claim to ship everywhere on the world, but both fall a little short once you start getting away from major hubs in developing countries. They cover this by saying they ship to their hub, and hold the items for pick up - but that's not helpful when your engine is broken and the hub is 800 miles away.

While it's a bit overkill, you can also use shipping agencies like these for paperwork and documents you need while on the road (like registration renewals). It's more expensive than regular mail, but has improved tracking features and (again, if you've asked around), you know it will be delivered to where you are. Hopefully, with things like documents, you've planned ahead enough to have them mailed somewhere which can accept them and hold them until you get there, but we all make mistakes on timing. Keep this alternative in mind when you need something *right away.*

In Closing

It's hard to be exhaustive on a topic as large as learning to be an overland traveler. There is no real way to judge what's needed for each traveler, each vehicle, each trip. Some people never want to cross an international border (but still spend a long time on the road), others can't wait.

So, if I missed something you think is vital, or something you feel you need to know and didn't learn in this book, then please contact me and let me know (contact information below). I'm never above changing or adding or correcting things. That is part of learning, and learning is one of the most important skills for any Overlander.

I do hope, now that you've reached the end of this book, you have a better idea of what *you* need for *your* trip - and if you weren't sure you could do a such a trip, now you feel like you can. That was my goal when I started writing - to get answers to people who wanted to travel overland but weren't sure about the "how". How to do this or that thing, which ends up being simple once you've done it but is terrifying (or at least intimidating) before.

Some of you might have already done *big* trips, and read this just to see if there was something to learn. You might have learned something, I have no way of knowing, but one thing I do know is that I am always picking up tips and tricks from other travelers, allowing me to travel better, more easily, or just to somewhere I hadn't known existed until I heard about it.

I guess that is the last point I want to make. Now that you've read this book, go somewhere. Somewhere new to you, somewhere that challenges your comfort level. It doesn't matter whether you go alone or with friends, or even whether you go on a motorcycle or a bike or a truck, or even fly and rent a car or take a bus. See something you haven't seen, meet people you haven't met. The world is amazing and awesome, and full of people who will be glad to see you. All *you* have to do is get out there. Just Go.

About the Author

Andrew Pain started riding motorcycles against the fervent wishes of his mother in 1993. He has wanted to be a writer ever since he had a terrible math teacher in 7th grade, which probably kept him from a nice comfortable job as an accountant somewhere.

Having now traveled two continents in two hemispheres and broken more mechanical parts then he know vehicles actually had, he spends part of every year attending events and encouraging others to travel. He is particularly focused on getting Americans out of their own borders to see that the world is far less dangerous and far more wonderful than their televisions want them to believe.

He recently married a wonderful, strong woman, and they are planning to take off on motorcycles to see the world together.

www.ingramcontent.com/pod-product-compliance
Lightning Source LLC
Chambersburg PA
CBHW060331100426

42812CB00003B/955